Adam Smith and Yan Fu: Western Economics in Chinese Perspective

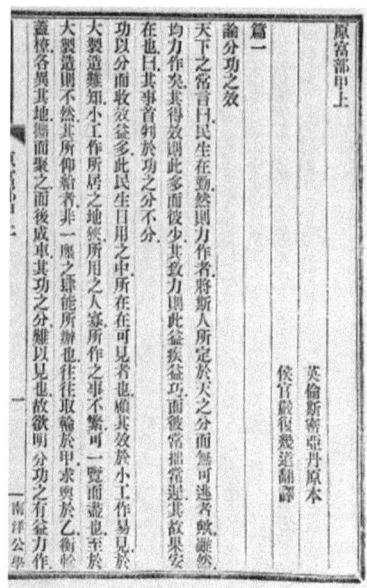

Yan Fu's translation of *The Wealth of Nations*, cover and first page (1902)

Cheng-chung Lai

Adam Smith and Yan Fu: Western Economics in Chinese Perspective

 Springer

Cheng-chung Lai
Emeritus Professor
Department of Economics
National Tsing Hua University
Hsinchu, Taiwan

ISBN 978-981-19-6572-2   ISBN 978-981-19-6573-9 (eBook)
https://doi.org/10.1007/978-981-19-6573-9

Translation from the Chinese language edition: 亞當史密斯與嚴復:《國富論》與中國 (*Adam Smith and Yan Fu: The Wealth of Nations and China*) by Cheng-chung Lai, © San Min Book 2002, Taipei, Taiwan. All Rights Reserved.
© San Min Book Co., Ltd. 2022
This work is subject to copyright. All rights are solely and exclusively licensed by the Publisher, whether the whole or part of the material is concerned, specifically the rights of reprinting, reuse of illustrations, recitation, broadcasting, reproduction on microfilms or in any other physical way, and transmission or information storage and retrieval, electronic adaptation, computer software, or by similar or dissimilar methodology now known or hereafter developed.
The use of general descriptive names, registered names, trademarks, service marks, etc. in this publication does not imply, even in the absence of a specific statement, that such names are exempt from the relevant protective laws and regulations and therefore free for general use.
The publisher, the authors, and the editors are safe to assume that the advice and information in this book are believed to be true and accurate at the date of publication. Neither the publisher nor the authors or the editors give a warranty, expressed or implied, with respect to the material contained herein or for any errors or omissions that may have been made. The publisher remains neutral with regard to jurisdictional claims in published maps and institutional affiliations.

This Springer imprint is published by the registered company Springer Nature Singapore Pte Ltd.
The registered company address is: 152 Beach Road, #21-01/04 Gateway East, Singapore 189721, Singapore

Acknowledgements

This English adaption is based on a Chinese version 亚当史密斯与严复:《国富论》与中国, 台北: 三民书局, 2002; 浙江大学出版社, 2009; 上海格致出版社, 2023. I am grateful to San Min Book (Taipei, Taiwan), the original 2002 publisher of this book, for the permission of this adaption.

I try to render it in a style suitable for Western readers by omitting Chinese-specific issues and add examples from Yan Fu's translations and comments, side by side with Adam Smith's original texts. As the main messages remain unchanged and new studies on this topic were limited, I only made minor updates and revisions.

Major parts of the first four chapters are taken from the following three papers: (1) "Adam Smith and Yan Fu: Western Economics in Chinese Perspective," *Journal of European Economic History*, 1989, 18(2):371–82. (2) "Translations of **The Wealth of Nations**," *Journal of European Economic History*, 1996, 25(2):467–500. (3) "Receptions of **The Wealth of Nations**," *The European Legacy*, 1996, 1(7):2069–83. These three papers were also appeared in *Adam Smith across Nations: Translations and Receptions of **The Wealth of Nations***, Oxford University Press, 2000, slightly revised as two Overviews and Sect. 1.2.

With generous supports from the Harvard-Yenching Institute (1992–3), I used the *Vanderblue Memorial Collection of Smithiana* (located at the Kress Library, Baker Library of Harvard Business School) to work out *Adam Smith across Nations* (2000). Chapters 2 and 3 in the present monograph are based on its two overviews.

For recent related studies, there is a mini-symposium "Adam Smith in international context" in *Adam Smith Review*, Volume 9, 2017. It contains one paper on Germany and two on China. Google Search shows that there are a few new papers on "Smith and Yan Fu" (in English); they are mostly on the cultural and translation aspects, not on economic issues.

Contents

1 Overview 1
   1 Proposition and Framework 1
   2 Yan Fu Studies 4
   3 Life and Times of Yan Fu 5
   4 Translation and Publication 6

2 Spread of *The Wealth of Nations* 9
   1 Adam Smith's Economic Doctrines 9
   2 Contents of *The Wealth of Nations* 11
   3 Translations of WN 12
       3.1 Introduction 14
       3.2 Speed and Number of Translations 14
       3.3 Quality of Translation 17

3 Receptions of *The Wealth of Nations* 21
   1 Method of Analysis 21
   2 Motives for Introducing WN 23
   3 Methods of Transmission 24
   4 Receptions 25
       4.1 Difficulties of Reception 25
       4.2 Impact on Decision-Makers 26
       4.3 Free Trade and Laissez-Faire 27
       4.4 Lack of Interest in Smithian Theory 28
       4.5 Reception By Left-Wing Readers 29
   5 Objections 30
   6 Smith's Impact in Retrospect 31

4 Traduttore Traditore 33
   1 Motivation of Translation 34
   2 Misunderstanding and Distortion 35
   3 The 310 Translator's Notes 37

5 Yan Fu's Understanding of *The Wealth of Nations* 41
1 General Economic Arguments 41
1.1 Pasture Yields As Good a Rent As Corn Land, and Sometimes a Greater One 41
1.2 On the Determination of the Value of Gold and Silver 42
1.3 Interest Rates and Precious Metals 44
1.4 The Fall in the Price of Corn Since the Establishment of the Bounty is Due to Other Causes 45
1.5 On Mercantilism 46
2 Criticisms on Smith's Doctrines 46
2.1 Theories of Rent 46
2.2 Law of Supply and Demand 49
2.3 Corn as Standard of Value 50
2.4 Navigation Acts 51
2.5 Meaningless Passages 51
3 Praises for Smith's Analyses 52
3.1 Basic Attitude 52
3.2 Anti-bullionism 52
3.3 On Monopoly 52
3.4 Some Defects 53

6 Yan Fu's Economic Ideas 55
1 Problems of Chinese Economy 55
1.1 Silver Standard 55
1.2 Lack of Standard in Measures and Specifications 57
1.3 Trade Deficits 58
1.4 Tax Corruption 58
1.5 Public Debt 59
2 Economic Liberalism 60
2.1 Anti-protectionism 60
2.2 Anti-monopoly 61
2.3 Economic Liberalism 63
3 Other Comments 64
3.1 Anti-commerce and Pro-agriculture 64
3.2 Saving or Prodigality? 65
3.3 War and Economy 66
3.4 Economic Mentality of the Mandarins 67
4 Sources of Yan Fu's Ideas 67

7 Epilogue 69
1 Response 69
2 Evaluation 72
3 Final Remarks 74

Contents ix

Appendices 77
Appendix A: Foreword to the First Chinese Edition of *The Wealth of Nations* **(1901)** 77
Appendix B: Preface to the First Chinese Edition of *The Wealth of Nations* **(1901)** 82
Appendix C: Liang Qichao's Comments on *The Wealth of Nations* **(1902–4)** 84
References 91

About the Author

Cheng-chung Lai (lai@mx.nthu.edu.tw) is Emeritus Professor at National Tsing Hua University (Taiwan), with three decades of experience in teaching economic history and history of economics thought. His books in English include: *Adam Smith across Nations: Translations and Receptions of The Wealth of Nations*, Oxford University Press (2000); *Braudel's Historiography Reconsidered* (2004); *History of Economic Ideas in 20 Talks* (2022). He was educated in Taiwan (BA) and Belgium (MA), received his doctorate from École des Hautes Etudes en Sciences Sociales, Paris.

List of Tables

Chapter 1

| Table 1 | Yan Fu's translations (in chronological order of Chinese version) | 3 |

Chapter 2

Table 1	*The Wealth of Nations* and Yan Fu's translation	13
Table 2	*The Theory of Moral Sentiments* (1759) and *The Wealth of Nations* (1776): first translation and time lag from first publication in English	15
Table 3	Translations of *WN* in 18 languages	15

Chapter 4

| Table 1 | Yan Fu's 310 translator's notes by categories | 38 |

Chapter 1
Overview

The purpose of this study is twofold. First, at a static level, I examine how *The Wealth of Nations* (1776, hereafter WN) was introduced into China at the turn of the twentieth century (1902). The translation was not easy because the Chinese language at that time had insufficient vocabulary to introduce this unknown discipline from a completely different cultural system.[1] Second, in a dynamic socio-economic context, Yan Fu (1854–1921) had this book in mind as a prescription for China's "Wealth and Power". The question is: was WN, a book which advocates laissez-faire, free trade and minimum government, helpful for this peripheral economy?

1 Proposition and Framework

This introductory chapter explains central proposition and framework of each chapter, on the current state of Yan Fu studies, a brief background of his life and times and Yan Fu's version of WN.

Chapter 2 presents main economic ideas of Smith and the contents of WN; Smith's text and Yan Fu's version are compared to show how much of the book was omitted or abridged (Table 1 in Chap. 2). I also show how WN was translated into various languages over the past two centuries (Table 2 in Chap. 2).

A key issue of Chap. 3 is how these countries with very different economic conditions and modes of thought reacted to Smith's doctrines. Only with this international comparison can we understand better that the Chinese translations (three times before

---

[1] The first Western Economics translated into Chinese was Henry Fawcett (1863): *Manual of Political Economy*. It was orally explained by a professor of the Institute of Foreign Languages (Tongwenguan), W.A.P. Martin, written in Chinese by Wang Fengjao, and published in 1880 as *Policy of National Wealth* in three volumes.

the 1970s) and receptions of WN was nothing special: although there are some particular elements in the case of China, the basic features of "the WN effects" are also observed in other countries such as Germany, Japan and Russia.[2]

How WN was translated into Chinese? Yan Fu's higher education was Navy academy, first in Southern China and then at the Royal Naval College, Greenwich (1877–9). Why he was motivated to translate WN, this famous old book (1776) during 1897–1900? How he condensed its contents and expressed in the style of classical Chinese (without punctuation), that only limited readers can follow? This is the focus of Chap. 4.

What is particular in Chap. 4 is that he added 310 translator's notes to explain Smith's texts, to criticize Smith's ideas, to compare China's situations with that of UK, to offer his own judgments and suggestions (see Tables 1 in Chap. 2 and 1 in Chap. 4). So Yan Fu was not merely a translator, what he did is a kind of "interpretation through translation".

Based on these 310 notes, Chap. 5 investigates Yan Fu's understanding of WN. Examples: (1) How he understood Smith's key ideas such as "invisible hand theorem", "diamond-water paradox"; (2) How he criticized Smith doctrines; (3) How he praised Smith ideas.

Chap. 6 presents Yan Fu's own economic ideas, the main materials are, again, his 310 notes. (1) How he perceived China's economic problems? (2) How he understood liberalism and promoted Smith's laissez-faire policies for China? (3) How he suggested other policies for China's search of "wealth and power"?

The concluding Chap. 7 discusses the influence of Yan Fu's translations (of Western books) in general, and the reception of his WN in particular. Based on Yan Fu's version, Liang Qichao was a main commentator and diffuser of Smithian doctrines in China. Liang challenged the idea of adopting Smith's mid-18th-century UK economic liberalism into the weak Chinese economy around 1900s.

He offered a counter-argument that what China needed was not liberalism, but, paradoxically, the mercantilism that Smith was eager to against in Book IV of WN, for a simple reason: "wealth and power" were the primary aims of mercantilism, considering China's weak situation and Yan Fu's mentality of "search of wealth and power", mercantilism should be a far better prescription: protection of infant industries and develop national industries, etc.

I am in opinion with Liang. Why Yan Fu did not realize this "paradox"? Recent studies on Yan Fu's ideas of liberalism (Lin, 1983, Huang, 1998) show that his perception of liberalism was greatly diverged from that of the John Stuart Mill and Smithian tradition. I doubt whether Yan Fu was attracted by Smith's liberalism, or by the fascinating title of this book: *Wealth of Nations*! Some further remarks are offered to conclude this study.

Yan Fu's own Foreword and his mentor Wu Rulun's Preface to the Chinese version of WN are translated as two appendices. Appendix C is on Liang Qichao's comments

---

[2] If we have three books on "WN and Russia", "WN and Japan" and "WN and Germany", one will see that the case of "WN and China" is less striking than one might have thought.

of WN. These three sources are useful to understand how WN was understood by three major intellectuals around the 1900s.

Taken together, a key point of this book is to reexamine Yan Fu's economic ideas via modern economics perspective. Yan Fu had no systematic economic writings, and his ideas were embodied in his 310 notes (one may call them *extensive marginalia*) to WN. There is a term named "the Yan Fu phenomenon", which means how Western thoughts were introduced into China, and how Chinese readers reacted to these doctrines.

This is an old field but deserves new investigations. Yan Fu studies require novel analytical tools from various disciplines such as politics, sociology, law, philosophy, biology to do deeper studies on every book that Yan Fu translated, as Table 1 shows.

"Adam Smith and Yan Fu" is a significant subject for two reasons. (1) From the point of view of international spread of economic ideas, one is interested to know how WN was translated and received by a country which had very different way of thinking and very different economic conditions; the Chinese case may serve to compare with the translations and receptions of WN in other cultures. (2) For Chinese intellectuals, Yan Fu's version of WN is the first widely known book in Western economics. This famous book, translated by a remarkable person like Yan Fu during early stage of modern Chinese enlightenment, and translated in a particular

Table 1 Yan Fu's translations (in chronological order of Chinese version)

	Original author and time of translation	Title and year of the original version	Year of Chinese version
1	A. Michie (uncertain)	*Missionaries in China* (1892)	1899 (uncertain)
2	T.H. Huxley 1894?–96	*Evolution and Ethics and other Essays* (1894)	1898
3	Adam Smith 1897–1900	*An Inquiry into the Nature and Causes of the Wealth of Nations* (1776)	1902
4	H. Spencer 1898–1903	*The Study of Sociology* (1873)	1903
5	J.S. Mill 1899	*On Liberty* (1859)	1903
6	E. Jenks 1903	*A History of Politics* (1900)	1903
7	C.L.S. Montesquieu 1900?-	*De l'Esprit des lois* (1748)	1904–9
8	J.S. Mill 1900–2	*A System of Logic* (1843)	1905
9	W.S. Jevons 1908	*Primer of Logic* (1876)	1909

Source Author's compilation
It is said that he had translated 10 books, but this table is all I can find (the first one is not quite certain)

way (abridged, distorted and "interpretation through translation" in his 310 notes), is a significant example for the history of economic ideas.

2 Yan Fu Studies

Research on Yan Fu was continuous nowadays. There was a high tide during 1980–90 to collect his writings in five volumes (Wang Shi, 1986) and to reprint his translations by The Commercial Press in Shanghai (1931) and in Beijing (1981). There are several biographies, almost every aspect of his activities, ideas and translations were discussed, the following brief survey is to show some Yan Fu studies for further reading, all in Chinese.

(1) Biographies. There are several (and still increasing), with various qualities (some of them repeating others). A reliable sources is Wang Shi (1975), other biographies, less recommended, can be easily found in the References (with Chinese characters).

(2) Yan Fu's writings and translations. A most important source is the 5-volume *Yan Fu Ji* (*Collected Works of Yan Fu*) edited by Wang Shi (1986) containing his poetry, letters, essays, diary, some miscellaneous translations and selections of his translator's notes. Wang and Wang (1982: 153–67) chronically listed Yan Fu's activities, main writings and translations; Niou and Sun (1990: 464–97) listed various versions of his publications.

(3) Documents on Yan Fu. Wang and Wang (1982: 168–71) is an "Index of studies on Yan Fu", which was updated by Niou and Sun (1990: 503–17); most publications on Yan Fu before 1990 are contained in these two sources. Huang (1998) is a profound study on Yan Fu's understanding and critique of Mill's *On Liberty*, the references therein cited are comprehensive and updated. A good source to find papers on Yan Fu published in Taiwan is the "Periodical index" of The National Library (Taipei), http://www.ncl.edu.tw/. There are quite a few internet sources in China to search related journal papers.

(4) Economic aspect of Yan Fu. Researches in this aspect are quite limited, they are journal papers and textbook chapters, all published in China; no monograph with full-length treatment is available. As to journal papers, Lo (1978), Shi (1978), Ye (1980) and Yu (1994, 1995) provide some discussions on Yan Fu's economic thought. As to textbook chapters, Zhao and Yi (1980) have an overview, the most systematic and much more deeply analyzed is Hou and Wu (1983) in which they used 60 pages to interpret Yan Fu's economic ideas. Many of these studies were interpreted from Marxist perspective, while my approach is neoclassical (i.e., modern Western economics). It will be beneficial if one reads these studies from both angles. Schwartz (1964) is still the most important work (in English) on Yan Fu studies, although some of his views are debatable, it is arguably a classic. In Sect. 1 in Chap. 4 I will discuss Schwartz's Chap. 5 on WN in more detail.

3 Life and Times of Yan Fu

Yan Fu (1854–1921) was born in the Province of Fujian, Southeastern China, into a modest family. His father died when he was fourteen, and consequently the family could not afford his study in a traditional private school. By that time the Chinese government was suffering so much from the invasion by Western countries that they realized that a direct and efficient way was to import Western technology.[3] One of the measures was the founding of a Navy School in 1886 in Fujian. Yan Fu passed the exams as a first top student and was awarded full tuition and scholarship.

He thus shifted from a traditional local education to Western polytechnic. After some unexpected political disorders, he was finally sent to study in the Royal Naval College in Greenwich, March 1877 to August 1879. During this period his attention also extended to social, economic and political aspects. In short, he was an alert foreign student in many respects.

After returning to China in 1879, he served as a professor in the Naval School in Fujian, from which he had been graduated three years previously. The next year he was promoted to Dean of the Naval School near Peking, the capital. In 1890 he became the president of that School until 1900 when it was dissolved due to the Boxer Rebellion. Thus ends his period of teaching.

During this period he tried to pass the State Functionary Exams four times, but failed all (1885, 1888, 1889 and 1893). Depressed, he started to translate Western works in the hope that he could thereby awaken his ignorant compatriots. His translation career thus opened. He is said to have translated ten works between 1894 and 1914.[4]

Among them, it is no doubt that T.H. Huxley's *Evolution and Ethics* (1894) was the most influential, for a straightforward reason: the public was deeply frustrated by foreign invasions since the Opium wars (1840), the ideas of social Darwinism conveyed in Huxley's book (such as "survival of the fittest" and "natural selection") had a strong impact. Chinese readers were eager to take any necessary counter-action against foreign dominance. The influence of Huxley and the reputation of Yan Fu is thereafter established. Schwartz (1964: 22–41, Chap. 2 "The Early Years") provides some further details of Yan Fu's life and work.

---

[3] See Chap. 18 of Hsu (1983) "Late Ch'ing Intellectual, Social, and Economic Changes, with Special Reference to 1895–1911" for an interesting and concise review.

[4] See Table 1 above. There is an important book in this regard by Wang and Wang (1982), in which eight papers from different authors are collected with photos of the books that Yan Fu translated. Many useful information is provided including the works by and on Yan Fu. Niou and Sun (1990) also provide interesting photos and materials for further reading.

4 Translation and Publication

Yan Fu's translation was published in 1901–2 by Nanyan College (Nanyang Gongxue, now named Jiaotong University) in Shanghai in eight slim volumes. Its printing and binding style was traditional, a main characteristic is without punctuation. The Commercial Press (Shanghai) reprinted it in 1931 with old-style punctuation (i.e., showing stops of sentences, not modern punctuation with comma, period, semi-colon).

What is significant is that this 1931 edition has an 80-page glossary: showing difficult names and terms in Chinese with English, hoping that may help readers. Some brief explanations are added in this glossary, but in some cases the editors were hard to find the corresponding names and terms in English. This glossary indicates two main difficulties when reading Yan Fu's translation: culturally, there are barriers to understand Smith's messages and reasoning; technically, readers are further discouraged by the troubling names and terms that Yan Fu never explained.

This "Yan Fu translation series" by the Commercial Press (1931) contained eight Western books translated by Yan Fu, including WN (see Table 1). This series was reprinted by the Commercial Press (Taipei) in 1977, upon which the present study is based. WN in this series was a 3-volume set, pocket-size, 978 pages. The Commercial Press in Beijing reprinted this 1931 edition with new (Western) style punctuation, the glossary was also updated and printed as footnotes rather than endnotes. This new print facilitates readers greatly.

Hereunder is a brief account showing the process of Yan Fu's translation of WN and its publication. The main sources are his correspondence with his publisher Zhang Yuanji, who was editor-in-chief for the Nanyang College and the Commercial Press; this may also explain why all Yan Fu's translations were published there.

These 20 letters, all from Yan to Zhang, are reprinted in the *Collected Works of Yan Fu*, III: 524–57. Interested readers may find Yan Fu's correspondence with his Mentor Wu Rulun (III: 520–5, V: 1559–62) to see how Wu initially declined but finally agreed to write the Preface for WN. The page numbers cited below are all from these sources.

According the Yan's eldest son, he began the translation of WN in 1897 when aged 45 (V: 1545, 1548). We do not know in which month he began the work nor when he had such an idea. In the second letter to Zhang (25 February 1899), Yan stated that: "What you see is my translation of Adam Smith's book on the management of state finance. I am engaged it since more than a year but was interrupted by many other matters. That is why I have not yet completed half of it, otherwise it can be done in a year. I plan to complete it this year but heaven knows if I could do it" (III: 527).

This is the report Yan Fu made to his publisher a year after his engagement. In a letter of 3 July 1899, he reported that "I spend my leisure time to translate WN and by now I have done more than half of it. It counts more than twenty thousand words, I am employing someone to prepare a clear copy and will submit them to you. They are so copious that cannot be done within a short time" (III: 532). This shows the progress is satisfactory.

In a letter of 20 August 1899, he explained the importance of WN and his views: "This is an important book that one cannot afford not reading it if one wants to understand political economy. It is a foundation of political economy, it covers not only the principles of how to manage state finance and the national wealth of various countries, but also rich in the banking, industrial, commercial policies of Western countries. It provides also rich information about inter-continental trade since the Great Discovery. The reason why I choose this [old] book to translate, was not because I am not aware of recent books in political economy that are with finer analyses and more sophisticated arguments, it was mainly because what WN criticized are also major problems of Chinese economy" (III: 532–3).

Yan Fu was quite confident about his style as he stated in a letter of 2 February 1900: "I have done the first four Books of WN, I am now working on Book V concerning state expenditure and tax revenue. If not interrupted, all will be done by April. After this, I shall add a Forward, table of contents, translator's notes, and a brief account on Smith's life and work. ... It is really not easy to complete a book. As to translation, I am confident that I am one of the best in this country, but every time when I meet difficult sentences that contain profound messages, I always fall into puzzles, fighting with them all the time. Recently Mr. Wu told me that WN is the best book in political economy and that my translation with elegant and sharp style is useful to reveal the subtle ideas of WN; this translation will have an enduring value. Today's readers may not aware of this book, its publication in your College Press will be a leading event to provoke more translation of Western political economy books" (III: 537–8).

During 1900–1 some unexpected delays happened when copying and mailing the drafts; Yan Fu expressed his worries and impatience in several letters, but they were all finally resolved. In a letter of 5 February 1902, he was expected to see its publication: "I sent you the Preface by Wu [see Appendix B] last month and I suppose you have received it. Every visitor asks me if I could pass them a copy of the book, I am eager to see it in print. Send me twenty or thirty copies by mail" (III: 546). He said the same thing a month later: "Everybody asks me about the book, is that printed? Let me know by mail. If someone is coming up to the North, you may ask him to bring ten or twenty copies, I will pay the costs" (III: 551).

When published, a friend wrote to Yan Fu: "I read your translation of WN this May, ...the style is so elegant that one may wonder that it was done by an ancient scholar. ...I fancy that it would be nicer if this translation was in a more fluent style such that everybody can understand it better" (undated, V: 1571–2).

This is a representative reaction: Yan Fu's style is too difficult to follow; general readers need to fight with two hard things: Yan Fu's sentences and Smith's "unfamiliar" messages. Another friend wrote with an amusing tone: "Your WN that was just published sold out immediately, only very few can understand it. People buy it to put on the desk to show they are in touch with the 'new learning' [newly introduced Western knowledge]" (7 January 1903; V: 1574).

Chapter 2
Spread of *The Wealth of Nations*

When WN was published in 1776, it was immediately translated into German (1776) and French (1778) and other languages (Table 3); many countries had more than three versions (also Table 3). From the perspective of cross-nation transmission, Yan Fu's version (1902) was a late part of this "WN spread movement". To understand better the significance of WN in the Chinese world, we need a broader perspective.

(1) Doctrines of Smith's political economy and the significance of WN in Western economics, that is the subject of Sect 1.
(2) What are the contents of WN (Table 1)? Why it was read and printed over and over again since 1776? (Sect. 2).
(3) Over the past two centuries, WN was translated into how many languages and how many times? There must had some interesting things behind and happened (Sect. 3).
(4) Section 4 asks the following questions. Why these countries were eager to translate WN? How they reacted to Smithian doctrines? How readers from various ideological standings argued with Smith's liberalism? Did WN had significant impact on these non-English speaking countries?

These questions and answers are not directly related to "Adam Smith and Yan Fu", and this international comparison is useful to provide a wider perspective on the relative meaning of "WN and China".

1 Adam Smith's Economic Doctrines

Smith's writings are wide enough to cover moral philosophy (*The Theory of Moral Sentiments*), philosophy (*Essays on Philosophical Subjects*), rhetoric (*Lectures on Rhetoric and Belles Lettres*) and jurisprudence (*Lectures on Jurisprudence*); he is best known as father of modern political economy (economics) for WN (*An Inquiry into the Nature and Causes of the Wealth of Nations*).

In 1976 (bicentenary of WN) Oxford University Press (OUP) offered the famous *The Glasgow Edition of the Works and Correspondence of Adam Smith*, which is supposed to be an authoritative version. The long-awaited *The Life of Adam Smith* was finally available (Ross, 1995, revised 2010), also by OUP.

As to WN, the 1976 edition is much more complete and assimilated many information from the once-famous Cannan's definitive edition (1904). In the same year (1976) The University of Chicago reprinted the Cannan edition for three reasons, as George Stigler said in the Preface: "it is less encumbered with editorial material; it has useful marginal summaries of the text; and, as Smith would observe, it is a good deal cheaper".

So both editions prevailed in today's WN studies; I use the OUP 1976 edition for its informative footnotes provided by editors and for its complete index and related references. During Smith's lifetime WN had five editions (1776, 1778, 1784, 1786 and 1789), the 6th appeared in 1791, a year after his death. What Yan Fu based was the 1784 third edition, annotated by Professor Thorold Rogers (1823–90).

Among other things, WN is known for its liberalism (laissez-faire, laissez-passer) and anti-mercantilism (economic/commercial policies prevailed during sixteenth to eighteenth centuries). WN is regarded as the foundation of classical economics mainly because it was a first attempt to synthesize economic analyses in a unified framework. My main concern is more on Smith's specific ideas, so let us see first what is mercantilism. Two famous historians of European economic history Clough and Rapp (1975: 204) told us:

> To all the economic theory from 1500 until well into the eighteenth century has been given the generic term *mercantilism*. This lumping is unfortunate, for as we shall see presently, both economic theory and practice varied widely from place to place and changed through time. ... In brief, mercantilism in both theory and practice was economic state building and the use of the state to enhance the interests of policy makers, whether princes or private entrepreneurs.

This sounds what Yan Fu was searching for China. Why Smith was so against it? Because,

> The state intervene in all aspects of economic life, primarily by means of regulations to attain desired ends and to further the fortune of those who had political power and influence. ...Eventually, much of the state economic planning went awry, largely because it tried to keep alive uneconomic enterprises, because it curbed private initiative, because its red tape caused bitter hatred of the system, and because it engendered national rivalries which led to wars and the loss of the very purpose of the planning. ... The doctrines of *laisser faire* and of economic individualism were direct attacks upon mercantilism and mark the beginning of its end. (Clough and Rapp, 1975: 204–5)

The aim of mercantilism is what China needed around 1900; but its consequences are what China should avoid. If UK was a model to follow, should China follow mercantilism or Smithian *laissez-faire*? Could China afford the costs of mercantilism, or was China's backwardness suitable to adopt Smithian liberalism? Stated differently, was it a correct choice to translated WN as China's search of wealth and power? This will be discussed in Sect. 7.2.

Interpreting economic system from the perspective of 'natural law' was a new wave. Smith had two main intellectual affinities: he was a dear friend of David Hume (1711–76), a leading Scottish Enlightenment; he was in opinion with French Physiocrats such as Quesnay (promotor of *laissez-faire, laissez-passer*); he also interacted with intellectuals such as Voltaire, Rousseau and Turgot.

A famous metaphor in Smithian liberalism is the "invisible hand theorem", in which he advocates that, under a free society, while everybody pursuits his own interest, there is an invisible hand to coordinated their overall interests such that the benefits of the whole society will be greater. In other words, welfare is better-off in a *laissez-faire* society than in a planned, regulated mercantilist society. The "invisible hand" does better for citizens than the "visible foot" policy by mercantilists.

Smith was not against the aims mercantilism pursued, what he against was their intervention/regulation that led to disadvantages. Smith was not a nationalism nor a cosmopolitan, he was a rational defender of national interests; he advocated liberalism with a clear wish in mind: to increase the power and status of the UK.

Smithian economics can be simplified into three points. (1) The basic motive of human economic activity is self-interest. (2) He assumed there existed a natural law in the operation of economic system (as in the universe); this natural law functions like an invisible hand, will coordinate various interests to maximize social welfare. (3) To reach this goal, a most simple and efficient way is *laissez-faire* (liberalism or non-interventionism). Functions of the government are limited to army, justice (law enforcement), public construction and the maintenance of public system (such as education).

The above three points are certainly not what China was eager to learn in 1900, when facing foreign invasions and economic crises. I doubt Yan Fu had good understanding of these characteristics in WN, otherwise how could he introduce WN to readers who were mostly in the Confucian tradition (against self-interest) and eagerly welcomed the Darwinian idea of "survival of the fittest"?

2 Contents of *The Wealth of Nations*

Table 1 summarizes the structure of WN. It has five Books, each has 11, 5, 4, 9, 3 chapters respectively. At the end of Book I (i.e., Chap. 11), there is a lengthy "Digression concerning the Variations in the Value of Silver during the Course of the Four last centuries" (Smith, 1976: 195–275), which is included in Chap. 11 of Table 1 because Yan Fu did so.

In my pocket size edition, a page in Chinese contains approximately 60% of the contents of the page in the English version. In addition, the 310 translator's notes account for about 14% of the total space in Chinese version. This means Yan Fu translated about 46% of WN. If one says that Yan Fu's elegant classical style used less words than modern Chinese, it is still fair to say that he translated only 50–60% of the whole material.

In his Foreword Yan Fu claimed to have translated every chapter of WN, except two passages: one is, as mentioned above, immediately after Part III, Chapter XI of Book I: "Digression concerning the variations in the value of silver during the course of the last four centuries", he did summaries rather than translation for this lengthy appendix. The other is "Digression concerning banks of deposit, particularly concerning that of Amsterdam" (Chapter III of Book IV, Smith, 1976: 479–88). He considered both subjects are irrelevant to Chinese readers.

He did translate every chapter and every section, but very often rewrote the text in a condensed form. This method is not so unusual in the nineteenth century, in China as well as in other countries. The version on which he based was the third version of WN (1784) commented and footnoted by Professor Thorold Rogers (1823–90). He frequently mentioned Roger's opinions in his translator's notes (see Table 1 in Chap. 4).

The total pages of each Chapter and each Book of WN are listed in Table 1, to show their proportions and to compare their corresponding pages. One can also see how many translator's notes Yan Fu added. For instance, Smith's Chaps. 1–3 of Book I contain 21 pages, Yan Fu condensed them into 18 pages (in a small-size book). But in Chap. 8 "wages of labour" Yan Fu used 40 pages, much longer than Smith's 23 pages.[1]

3 Translations of WN[2]

> So the study of economic processes must include the study of economists, or of the origin, flow, and development of their ideas—for one can hardly separate the study of the origin of ideas from that of the change and flow of ideas. Such a study includes as well as all the processes of changes in ideas, and how ideas originate, also the processes by which they succeed, catch on, and dominate their time; it includes also the lags and impediments in the flow of ideas, both across and within national and linguistic frontiers.
>
> T. W. Hutchison: "Insularity and Cosmopolitanism in Economic Ideas, 1870–1914",
> *American Economic Review*, 1955, 45(2), p. 1.

---

[1] For excellent chapters related to mercantilism and Smith, I would like to recommend Blaug (1997, for advanced readers) and Ekelund and Hébert (1997, for general readers).

[2] This section and Chap. 3 on the translations and receptions of WN are condensed from Lai (1996, 1996a). One thing deserves mention. In the 18 appendix tables (Lai, 1996: 478–500), I displayed detail information on various editions and printings of WN in 18 languages (for the names of these countries, see Table 3): on the translator's names, translated titles, year of publication, volumes, pages and specific features of these editions/printings. These tables are strong evidence to show the spread of WN across nations over the past two centuries.

3 Translations of WN

Table 1 *The Wealth of Nations* and Yan Fu's translation

	Contents	Original pages	Yan Fu's pages	No. of Yan Fu's notes
Book I	Factor productivities and factor Income distribution	258	276	116
Chapter	1–3 Division of labour	21	18	4
	4 Origin and use of money	8	5	3
	5–7 Prices of commodities, etc.	34	41	17
	8 Wages of labour	23	40	16
	9 Profit of stock	12	18	8
	10 Wages of profits in labour and stock	45	54	24
	11 Rent of land	115	110	44
Book II	The nature, accumulation, employment of stock	98	98	39
Chapter	1 Division of stock	8	9	3
	2 Money as instrument of circulation	46	42	12
	3 Accumulation of capital	20	22	11
	4 Stock lent at interest	9	9	3
	5 Different employment of capitals	15	16	10
Book III	Different progress of opulence in different nations	42	34	12
Chapter	1 Nature and progress of opulence	6	5	1
	2 Discouragement of agriculture in Europe	12	14	5
	3 Rise and progress of cities and towns	11	10	2
	4 Contributions of towns commerce to the country	13	16	4
Book IV	System of political economy	256	267	64
Chapter	1 Mercantile system	23	27	6
	2–6 Free trade	103	100	31
	7 Colonies	84	95	20
	8 Conclusions of the mercantile system	20	20	3
	9 Physiocratic system	26	25	3

(continued)

Table 1 (continued)

	Contents	Original pages	Yan Fu's pages	No. of Yan Fu's notes
Book V	Revenue of the nation	248	293	79
Chapter	1 National expenditure	116	149	42
	2 National revenue	90	97	30
	3 Public debts	42	47	7

Note One page of Yan Fu's translation corresponds approximately to the half page of Smith's original version. *Sources* The Cannan edition of *The Wealth of Nations* (1902), Modern Library version; and from Yan Fu's 1902 translation, Taipei: The Commercial Press, 3 volumes (reprinted)

3.1 Introduction

WN is an example par excellence for studying the international transmission of ideas; it has been read (or at least mentioned) for more than two centuries; and it is still being read, in many different ways, around the world regardless of ideological background. This could be, along with *Das Kapital*, the most translated, although not necessarily the most read, economics book in history.

Translations of WN must be put in a wider framework of intellectual movement, to locate its significance within that context, in a dynamic perspective. For example, the first Italian version in Naples (1790) may be regarded as evidence of the intense participation of Italian scholarship in the general European cultural renewal movement, or more broadly speaking, a signal of participating the Enlightenment movement.

Why WN was soon translated into major languages could be due to Smith's previous book, *The Theory of Moral Sentiments* (TMS, 1759), was well received by the intellectual community. Recall that political economy was not an important discipline in the eighteenth century, while Moral Philosophy (or generally speaking, Scottish Enlightenment) was.

3.2 Speed and Number of Translations

Table 2 shows the spread of TMS and WN in five countries: in every case the time lag between the English edition and the translation is much shorter for WN than for TMS (columns 3 and 5). There are two patterns: (1) in the cases of France and Germany, TMS was well known and well received, that paved the way for WN (see column 5, time lag: 2 and 0 years). (2) In Russia, Spain and Japan, where WN was better-known, TMS was translated much later than WN (see column 7: 66, 149, 78 years respectively).

That is because France and Germany translated WN just as they did TMS, from an intellectual perspective. While Russia, Spain and Japan (then developing countries) were mainly interested in learning something useful from "the nature and causes

Table 2 *The Theory of Moral Sentiments* (1759) and *The Wealth of Nations* (1776): first translation and time lag from first publication in English

Language (1)	First translation of TMS published (2)	Time lag (years) (3)	First translation of WN published (4)	Time lag (years) (5)	TMS earlier than WN (years) (6)	TMS later than WN (years) (7)
French	1764	5	1778	2	14	
German	1770	11	1776	0		
Russian	1868	109	1802	26		66
Spanish	1941	182	1792	16		149
Japanese	1948–9	189	1870	94		78

Source For *the theory of moral sentiments* (*TMS*), see the introduction to the 1976 Oxford University Press edition, pp. 32–3. For *WN*, see Table 3

Table 3 Translations of *WN* in 18 languages

(a) First translation (regardless of whether full or abridged)		(b) Number of full and partial translations in each country	
Year	Language	Time(s)	Country
1776	German	14	Japan
1778	French	10	Germany
1779	Danish	6	Italy
1790	Italian	6	Russia
1792	Spanish	6	Spin
1796	Dutch	5	France
1800	Swedish	5	Sweden
1802	Russian	3	China
1811	Portuguese	3	Korea
1870	Japanese	2	Denmark
1902	Chinese	2	Poland
1927	Polish	2	Portugal
1928	Czech	2	Romania
1933	Finnish	1	Czechoslovakia
1934	Romanian	1	Egypt
1948	Turkish	1	Finland
1957	Korean	1	Holland
1959	Arabic	1	Turkey

Note As of 1993, author's compilation. Each country needs to be updated, for instance, by 2020 Chinese version almost reached to 10

of the wealth of nations" at the outset, then realized that TMS was an important philosophical foundation for a better understanding of WN.

Table 3 offers information about the speed and number of translating WN (as of early 1990s). Although WN has been translated into 18 languages, this is a small portion compared with modern living languages. Of course the reading population covered by these 18 languages is actually large enough. Among the Asian languages, there were no translations in Thai, Malay and others; the same is true of many Indo-European languages.

Second, countries with fewer than five or six editions seem "normal". Two unusual cases are Germany and Japan: why were (are) they so mad about WN, unsatisfied by previous translations, doing it over and over again, generation after generation? In the case of Germany, the famous F. List had harsh criticism for WN, but why they are still obsessed with WN? In Japan, there were 14 translations, partly because they have translated from various English editions, with or without Cannan's copious notes. Perhaps Japan has the highest proportion of economists involved in Smith studies.

Third, this translation movement continues nowadays. There are new Danish, French, Korean and Spanish translations in progress. The Chinese versions increased since the 1990s could be have 10 in total around 2020. Data of other countries also need to be updated.

Fourth, if we take countries with more than three translations and look at the time distribution, we will see that in China it was between 1900 and 1930s, then another new wave in the 1990s–2010s. Korea in the 1950s–1970s; France in the 1770s–1820s; Sweden in the 1800s; Italy in the 1790s–1850s and from 1945 to 1976; Russia in the 1800s–1930s (quite evenly). Germany, Japan and Spain all show a continuous interest.

Fifth, by contrast, where there is only one translation it is generally a partial, selective or abridged. Why were these countries less passionate? Because most intellectuals can read either English or other major-language, this may explain why there is no complete Swedish translation and why Japan has so many translations (most readers are not familiar with academic English). But this cannot explain the case of Germany, where a high percentage of intellectuals are familiar with English.

In terms of speed of translation, there is an interesting anecdote on the competition of translating WN. In the *Mémoires de l'Abbé Morellet* (1823), Morellet states that he spent the autumn of 1776 in Champagne (France) and occupied himself assiduously in translating WN.

Almost at the same time, Abbé Blavet (an ex-Benedictine, who translated TMS in 1774) also translated WN and sent in weekly installments to the *Journal de l'agriculture…* Blavet's work was appeared from January 1779 to December 1780, then reprinted in six volumes in Yverdon (Switzerland) and in Paris, both in 1781.

Morellet complained that this "proved an obstacle to the publication of mine. I was offered it for a hundred louis, and then for nothing, but the competition caused its rejection." He was rejected once more by Archbishop of Sens and complained that "poor Smith was traduced rather than translated. … My translation was carefully made. Everything of an abstract character in Smith's theory becomes unintelligible in Blavet's translation, but in mine may be read with profit."

3 Translations of WN   17

Blavet's translation was supported by Smith. In his letter (No. 218 in the *Correspondence of Adam Smith*, OUP 1976) to Blavet dated 23 July 1782, sent from Edinburgh, Smith said that he was very pleased by Blavet's previous translation of TMS and "I am even more pleased by the way you have done for my latest work [WN] …I found your translation is, in all aspects, perfectly equal to the original… I am personally so obliged to you, that I cannot encourage or favor another translation." (my translation).

To my knowledge, this is the only case of direct competition; translations of WN also competed in Japan but that was the competition in quality and among different editions, not between translations done at the same time.

3.3 Quality of Translation

Some interesting things happened during this translation movement. There were problems of "false edition" and "unidentified edition"; problem of censorship in Spain; problems of misunderstanding and distortion, there are more cases beyond my knowledge.

3.3.1 False and Unidentified Editions

By "false edition" I mean the translator claims that he worked from the original English edition while in fact it was re-translated from an edition in other language. In the first Italian edition (1790), the translator claimed that was based Smith's, but it was based on Blavet's 1779–80 French version.

The first Spanish version (1792) was an expurgated translation of Condorcet's synopsis of WN, which was appeared in French in the *Bibliothque de l'homme public*, III (108–216) & IV (3–115), published in Paris (1790). The translator "not only suppressed or garbled parts of Condorcet's work but failed to identify the original as the work of Smith."

A case of unidentified edition. The first French translation was published in 1778–9 in The Hague, Netherlands with the translator's name given as "M***". Another French edition was published in Paris in 1781, the translator's name was not given but it was generally acknowledged that he was l'Abb Blavet. Many people considered that the Paris (1781) and The Hague (1778–9) editions were by the same translator but printed in different places in different formats: one in three volumes, the other in four.

M. Guyot of Neufchâtel wrote to Blavet in 1778 that when the edition of 1778 appeared, he and Douglad Stewart believed that it was done by Abb Morellet. However, by comparing the two translations, Murray concluded that "The Hague translation was thus a year earlier in date, and was evidently by a different hand." This conclusion still does not answer the question of who was the translator of the 1778–9 The Hague edition.

3.3.2 Censorship

The first Spanish translation by Carlos Martnez de Irujo (Oficial de la Primera Secretara de Estado) was an expurgated translation of Condorcet's synopsis. The "Inquisition" banned the original (French) version on 3 March 1792, but permitted an extract to be published in Spanish (1792). Writing from Munich in December 1792, Sir John Macpherson told Edward Gibbon that the Spanish government had "permitted an extract of Adam Smith's *Wealth of Nations* to be published, though the original is condemned by the Inquisition". The translator assured "that he had deleted everything which could induce error or relaxation on religious and moral matters".

This censorship continued to the first complete Spanish translation (1794), by Jos Alonso Ortz. This was probably based on the 5th (1789) edition, but Ortz thought it was the 8th edition (impossible because the 8th edition was in 1796). Some sections were omitted. The translator was a lawyer attached to the royal councils and chancery in Valladolid and a professor of canon law and sacred theology.

On 15 February 1793, Ortz appeared before the Inquisition, explaining that some time ago he translated WN, "purging it of various impious proposals ... and eliminating entirely an article ... in which the author favors tolerance on points of religion, so that it stands cleansed of anything that could lead to error or relaxation in moral and religious matters."

The Supreme Council of the Inquisition sent Ortz's translation to three examiners (calificadores) on 16 February 1793, but the Inquisition was not satisfied with the opinion of two censors because Ortz's work avoided the errors of the French text. Curiously, it was never suggested that Ortz's translation be collated with the English text; the French version was repeatedly referred as the "original", see Smith (1976: 122).

On 29 May, the Inquisition named a new panel of examiners, including the friar who had condemned the French translation. After some minor revisions made by Ortz, the manuscript was returned to him on 22 October, then published in 1794 with permission.

3.3.3 Traduttore Traditore

Examples of rewriting rather than faithfully translating are abundant. The case of Chinese edition (1902) is a living example. Yan Fu in fact did as much rewriting as translating not to mention his heavy abridgment (about 54% of Smith's text was "translated"). His reasons may have been that the whole book is too long for a complete translation; even within the parts translated, there are many digressions in Smith's text that the translator judged of little interest (e.g., the history of wheat price in London in the Appendix of Book I).

Problems of misunderstanding and distortion are more serious when WN is translated into different cultural systems (e.g., Chinese and Japanese) than into different languages (e.g., French, German). The case of China is a good example, because when WN was translated in 1899, the Chinese language had no sufficient vocabulary for many terms and concepts. Moreover, the analytical tools, methods of reasoning and historical background of WN were completely unfamiliar to readers.

There are many examples of this kind: Yan Fu translated "labor" into something like "ability" and could make no distinction between "productive and unproductive labor". More difficult still for Yan Fu are new concepts: how can induction, marginal productivity and stock be translated? In some cases, he tried to find similar terms from Chinese classic books; in some cases he simply skipped them; in some he invented new terms.

Despite the difficulties, he essentially transmitted Smith's main messages. I think he did better in Book IV and Book V, where concrete policies (anti-mercantilism, public finance problems) are argued and theoretical parts are less successful.

Similar misunderstandings and distortions also appeared in Japan. Professor Kenji Takeuchi, one of the most famous and serious translators of WN, translated it in 1921–3 and revised it in 1931–3. This edition is still in print and widely circulated today. After retired, in 1963 he published a book titled *Mistranslation*, in which he discusses the problems of misunderstanding in translating WN and Ricardo's *Principles of Political Economy and Taxation*. He criticized mistranslation by Japanese professors, commented on their "errors" and "ignorance", and said he was ashamed of such "ugly translations". He gave many examples showing how different professors have translated certain passages quite differently.

Reading this self-criticism, one understands why there are 14 translations of WN in Japan. If Japanese Smith scholars are so obsessed with perfection, they may have another 14 translations over the next two centuries. In terms of quality, Japan is number one in translating WN, their attention to details is incomparable.

In Spain, there was a higher-level "translation" of WN into exact science language. "Toward the end of the eighteenth century Ramn Campos, a physics professor and the author of works on logic, attempted to make the ideas of Smith better known through a text on economics reduced to exact, clear and simple principles." Adam Smith, he declared, "made himself immortal by the brilliance with which he presented the substance of Stewart's [sic] work."

It was Campos's ambition to publicize the findings of both economists, so that the science "so mysterious until now, may through my work become widely known, being universally accepted among the number of exact sciences." In eight short chapters of his La *Economia reducida a principos exactos, claros y sencillos* (Madrid, 1797), Campos covered concisely, but accurately, the Smithian theories of prices, wages, profit, capital, and taxation; and he devoted an appendix to public debts. It is not clear for whom the miniature volume was intended or how widely it was read.

It may be doubted that Campos fulfilled his declared purpose of making economics "universally accepted among the number of exact sciences". For modern Smithian scholars, it would be amazing to re-examine Campos's method of translation, his analytical tool and his achievements; he could be one of the first mathematical economists in the history of economic analysis.

Translation is a neglected part of transmission of economic ideas; the problems of misunderstanding and distortion is an important but unexplored territory. When the translation problem is put in an international comparative framework, many interesting phenomena appear. We will be able to draw a better picture of the spread of WN across nations only when more in-depth individual country case studies become available.

Chapter 3
Receptions of *The Wealth of Nations*

> When a given body of information passes the national frontiers it acquires a new complexion, a new national, cultural physiognomy.
>
> Thorstein Veblen [re-quoted from Spengler (1970):
> *History of Political Economy*, 2(1):133.

This chapter surveys how ten non-English speaking countries (China, Denmark, France, Germany, Italy, Japan, Portugal, Russia, Spain and Sweden) reacted to Smithian ideas. I focus on the following topics: the motives and methods through which WN was introduced; how Smith's basic proposals such as free trade were received; the nature of objections to Smith's doctrines. I reached a conclusion: Smith's impact outside English-speaking countries was mainly at the level of ideas; his influence on policies was not observed.

1 Method of Analysis

My aim is to present a picture of the international transmission of economic ideas, the language barrier is obvious but of secondary importance, for the real difficulty lies in having a good knowledge of the situations and currents of thought in these countries, to understand the nature of the receptions and the objections of WN. The combination of both difficulties (language and economic history knowledge) set heavy constraints.

Taking Germany as an example. WN was translated in 1776, the same year as the first English edition came out, while the newest German edition (as of 1993) was 1974. The contents of WN did not change much in various editions but the situation and thought (mentality) in Germany have been changed radically. Because of this dynamic change, it would be a challenging task to write a systematic study on the receptions of WN in Germany over the past two centuries.

WN in Russia also has a telling story: Smith's main ideas and policy proposals had already spread among intellectuals and decision makers at least eight years before

WN was published (1776), one also observe a "rise and fall" of Smithianism in Russia. Given this complexity within a single country, I have to ask myself whether it is possible to handle ten countries simultaneously in one essay.

What I am offering is a general (and mosaic) picture. Although the time-span I am looking at is quite vast, I shall focus more on the *early* receptions (eighteenth to nineteenth centuries) than on the recent (twentieth century). This kind of cross-country comparison is necessarily factual and fragmentary, but a first step must be set forward.

I can also only concern with the "external" aspects of the reception problem. That is, I can only deal with the "economic affairs" expressed in WN and the reception/debate of these policies. The "internal" aspect, such as Smith's theory of value, invisible hand theorem, self-interest, market efficiency, also caused discussions in these countries and had impacts on important thinkers such as Marx and many others. These internal aspects are much more delicate and harder to tackle for a cross-country comparison.

In his study on the introduction of Smith into the Continent (mainly focused on France, Germany and Italy), Palyi (1928: 180) begins by stating three difficulties in analyzing the issue. First, who could dare to say exactly how much of Smith's apparent influence on the Continental free trade movement was in reality due to other liberal thinkers? Second, it is difficult to separate the practical influences from the scientific ones; economic thought affects both science and practice. Third, it is even more difficult to distinguish in what proportion his influence on the Continent was due to his ideas, and to what degree it was due to his style, and the charming personality it expressed.

My difficulties here are even greater: If Palyi needed 54 printed pages in the 1920s to handle three countries with a shorter time-span, a fuller analysis of ten countries with longer period needs much more space. Palyi (1928) is the first (perhaps still the only) comparative study of this kind. The case of Italy was treated marginally, and his study was not really comparative in a strict sense because he treated Germany and France in different sections, not comparing their similarities and differences.

By contrast, my comparative approach does not take an individual country as a unit of analysis; I deal with individual topics (such as "the motives for translating WN") to see the general patterns. After this kind of overview, I felt that individual country studies are badly needed.

As one can see from Palyi's footnotes, he used many documents including brochures, pamphlets, textbooks, encyclopedia published at different times. This was possible as he concentrated on three countries. I do not possess such rich documentation for all the ten countries analyzed here. Even if I had such rich data and if I could read all the languages, my knowledge would still be insufficient to understand the whole issue to the extent of being able to present a synthesis of Palyi's depth (he was particularly good in the case of Germany).

Attention should also be drawn to Sect. 5 (pp. 224–233) of Palyi's study in which he discusses the reception of Smith's theories (such as interest, wage, value, money, social philosophy, methodology). This section is less successful than the previous four ones because he covered too many topics in too few pages, with the result of forming opinions rather than arguments. This aspect, as it is so complicated, is beyond the scope here.

I rely heavily on secondary studies. The availability of these studies in each country varies greatly. Germany and Russia have more documentation in English than the cases of France, Italy, Japan and Spain, although these latter countries have rich literature in their own respective languages. China, Denmark, Portugal and Sweden have only very limited documentation in English that would be of use to comparison. This comparison unavoidably puts heavier weight on document-rich countries.

I can only select one or two examples to illustrate each topic in question. Some secondary issues such as receptions by general readers are excluded here. Another point is that this kind of survey is difficult to have a unified framework to grasp scattered materials, neither to have a hypothesis to verify.

2 Motives for Introducing WN

Four types of motives are identified. The first type is those countries that wanted to learn from England's experience (as a powerful empire) through WN. This motive is described by the subtitle of Schwartz (1964): *In Search of Wealth and Power*.

England was, in Russian's eyes, a symbol of superlative naval power, technology and engineering, its nascent manufacturing was admired and envied. The fact that WN was written in England by a sensible University of Glasgow professor (a friend of famous David Hume) added legitimacy to the thoughts in WN. A major difference between Russia and China is that Russian intellectuals and decision makers already knew the main ideas of WN before 1776. Chinese intellectuals heard of WN as late as 1902 (125 years later).

A second type of motive has more intellectual inclinations than practical purpose. The Danish translator Frants Dræbye was the tutor of the Norwegian merchant James Collett's two sons. He took a trip with Collett's sons through several European countries, a trip which brought them to England in 1776 when WN just published, a book that was an important subject of conversation. Dræbye got the desire to acquaint the Danish and Norwegian readers with such a significant and much discussed work.

In the case of France, readers were interested mainly for intellectual reasons. The free trade policy and laissez-faire principle, that Smith so emphasized, was partly originated from French physiocrats. The level of understanding was different: Denmark was in a position of "learning" while France was in a position of scientific discourse.

A third type is strongly free trade inclined. A few Portuguese texts written between 1792 and 1802 contain scattered references to WN, nearly always concerning the division of labor and freedom of production and trade. The increasing audience for laissez-faire was a strong incentive for a wider diffusion of WN. In the short introduction to the first Portuguese edition (1811), Lisboa explains the importance of the translation for the understanding of the profound changes that were taking place in Brazil (where he lived). The significance of WN was the principles of laissez-faire, taking into account the liberalization of Brazil's economy.

A fourth type is Japan, combining the above three. WN was translated at one time in conjunction with practical need for free trade policy, and at another time from a purely scholarly point of view. Especially after the First World War, great importance was attached to WN as the source of social and economic ideas, it was also evaluated in connection with the socialist thought and it is from this particular viewpoint that a new Japanese translation was attempted. It is not that the one and the same WN was translated in various ways according to different social backgrounds and social needs, but it may be that the attempt to read WN from those points of view naturally led Japanese to recast their versions.

3 Methods of Transmission

Alexandrin (1977) offers an interesting framework for the analysis of this topic. He focused on the transmission and reception of WN in early Russia, proposing a framework to study the relationship among the five players: source–admirer–medium–transmitter–receptor. He then lists policies suggested by Smith (his Table 1) and policy interests of Russia (his Table 2) to investigate the real effect of the reception. I find the framework attractive and the perspective instructive; the Russian case serves as an ideal-type. I have no sufficient information to apply this framework to other countries, I shall present three different ways.

The first way considered is to translate WN by translators who either knew Smith personally (in the case of Denmark, Frants Dræbye), or who had correspondence with him and had obtained his authorization (in the case of France, Abb Blavet), or who had studied in England (in the case of China, Yan Fu). This is transmitting at the first level, a linear method of transmission.

Russia shows another way, a curvilinear one: through different channels in a same period. Two Russians students were at Glasgow University studied with Smith, bring his ideas to Russia. Amongst the Smith followers: Desnitsky, Tretyakov, Countess Catherine Dashkov, née Vorontsov and her very young son Paul (1763–1807); Count Mordinov, who was sent to London to "specialize"; and Count Vorontsov, Russian ambassador to the court of St. James (Alexandrin, 1977:2–3).

A third type happened at a different level: assimilation of WN into one's own economic discourse. Sartorius produced the first "Smithian textbook" in 1796: *Handbuch des Staatswirtschaft zum Gebrauche bey akademischen Vorlesungen, nach Adam Smith's Grundstzen ausgearbeitet*. He used this 234 pages textbook to teach at Göttingen University, and we find a précis of these advanced in WN, although the later sections show some sign of accommodation between Smith and traditional German treatment of *Staatwirtschaft*.

This textbook marked the beginning of a more positive reception of WN. Note that this textbook was translated into Swedish (1800). In his preface to this *Handbuch*, Sartorius says: "The author of the following summary has lectured for five years on the principles given here, and he is able to say that he has also been so fortunate as to make them comprehensive to beginners. The author is convinced that Smith has discovered the truth and he considers it his duty to contribute his share towards its dissemination".

Another example. The three-volume textbook of economics by K. H. Rau (1792–1870) remained the most widely used, many eminent German economists (Roscher, Wagner, C. Menger) were raised on it. It was published between 1826 and 1837, and numerous later editions followed. Rau incorporated Smithian doctrines into an older structure. It is fair to say that his textbook cannot claim analytical novelty, it smoothed the way for the reception of WN by incorporating its main ideas into traditional cameralistic discourse.

Two general barriers in transmitting WN: linguistic (insufficient vocabularies) and conceptual (lacking equivalent concepts). When WN appeared in Petersburg in four volumes (1802–6), the translation was a matter of great difficulty. The terminology of political economy was just being created. Social relations, analyzed by Smith, were still in many ways foreign to Russians.

The literary language of the Enlightenment was beginning to be translated, to fully discuss these subjects in Russian was almost impossible. By that time a "striking absence of both economic terms and business terminology" and only about "two dozen borrowed words which could be stretched to suit economic concepts", as Gerschenkron put it in *Europe in the Russian Mirror* (1970).

4 Receptions

Five topics are selected to illustrate this complicated issue: (1) the difficulties of reception; (2) WN's impact on decision makers; (3) free trade and laissez-faire as the most received message, a point that deserves detailed examination; (4) the lack of interest in Smith's theoretical discussion; (5) receptions by left-wing readers.

4.1 Difficulties of Reception

Two types of difficulties, the first one is obvious: general intellectual and economic environment in most receiving countries was not responsive to Smith's ideas. In Italy, under the mercantilist milieu of the 1780s, WN did not display a greater amount of common sense than the writings of leading Italian authors. WN even appeared as dogmatic and doctrinaire, on purely theoretical matters like value problem, and it was often less clear and less profound than the best Italian writings.

Consequently, even the few contemporary free traders hardly mentioned the book. The most influential one was the Neapolitan Gaetano Filangieri, in his rather able eclecticism of physiocratic principles and mercantilistic practices does not mention either Turgot or Smith, although his work came out later (1780) than WN (1776).

Even a pronounced free trader like the Count d'Arco (1739–91) of Mantova does not seem to know him. The Neapolitan Giuseppe Palmieri, presenting in 1790 a cautious treatment of commercial policy, does not reveal any influence of Smith; to him universal free trade or moderate protection were debatable alternatives (Palyi, 1928:189).

The second type of difficulties is less general, Prussia (Germany) was a good example to illustrate the resistance of Smithianism by another dominant current. It was not surprising that the cameralist professors whose textbooks were brought out in new editions even as late as the 1820s, often preferred to disregard WN. The book by Sonnenfels remained the official textbook of cameralism in the Austrian Empire until the revolution of 1848. His pupil, the Vienna professor von Kudler (1786–1853) did not have the courage until 1846 to pour a lot of Smithian spirit into the old stuff of his master.

Cameralistic resistance to Smith was a decisive one. The first response to Smithian liberalism was very unfriendly. The opposition found later its most characteristic literary expression in writings like Buesch and Rehberg (1754–1836), both under the influence of James Steuart (1712–90). Both were opposed to WN, though conceding some of its merits (Palyi, 1928:194–6).

4.2 *Impact on Decision-Makers*

Smith's impact on decision makers was limited. In France, as to financial matters, Napoleon's policy—he had read WN as well as Filangieri and Necker in the military school in Paris—of sound money and a stable interest rate, his severe economy in public expenditure, his distaste for public debts other than those of an emergency-character, and especially his decided attitude against every kind of direct state participation in trade, may have been suggested, partly at least, by Smith and his French followers (Palyi, 1928: 209). Yet this is far from a solid evidence.

The case of Russia is more concrete. Desnitsky, another Russian student who studied at Glasgow University, is regarded as one of the most outstanding able Russian social and political thinkers in second half of eighteenth century. He was seen both by pre-Revolutionary and by Soviet legal historians as the father of Russian jurisprudence. In 1767, Desnitsky wrote a remarkable *Predstavlenie* (Proposal concerning the Establishment of Legislative, Juridical and Executive Authorities in the Russian Empire) in response to the setting-up of Catherine II's Legislative Commission; he completed that work in 1768.

But the real influence was a different matter. Smith wrote about the functioning or the improvement of free, independent, established and operable economic units. Catherine II, on the other hand, was concerned with building the political, social and administrative basis of the infrastructure in her continent-sized kingdom. Although Catherine and her successor stated an intent to facilitate the creation of manufacturing and to aid the rise of the bourgeoisie, at the same time they continued enslaving people, monopolizing land (land for "well-born persons" only) and venting their reactionary views.

Catherine may have had enlightening thoughts but she was either incapable of understanding them, or could not pay attention to them in her actions, or, most likely, she saw their inapplicability in Russia at that time as for the future circumstances. She employed the ideas of the philosophers in a cynical way to further her ends. Smith's doctrine of free external trade and freedom in social and economic relations at home and abroad, never seemed influential in the Russian world (Alexandrin, 1977: 9–12).

4.3 Free Trade and Laissez-Faire

This principle was the best received part of WN, at least at the level of ideas. Every country received this message differently based on their own particular features.

In Italy, the most widely received ideas of Smith turned out to be, through Mengotti's work, the ideological of commercial freedom. That was mainly his free trade and laissez-faire ideas were of interest. This message was broadly accepted in its more or less radical guise. Around the 1840s, acceptance of Smith took root in Italian political and cultural terrain. Economic liberalism and free trade had became the means of uniting the most lively forces in the country. These joined together to form the Piemontese free-market movement, represented by an enthusiastic supporter of Smith's doctrines, the statistician Camillo Cavour.

In Portugal, a few Portuguese texts written between 1792 and 1802 contain scattered references to WN, nearly always concerning the division of labor and freedom in production and trade. Why Lisboa had a passion for Smith? It was Smith's clear-cut support of economic freedom. Lisboa was writing not in mainland Portugal, but in its chief colony, Brazil. Praise for WN also appears again and again in a group of pamphlets Lisboa published in Rio de Janeiro (1808–10).

His pamphlets were not merely a praise of the new economic measures in the colony; they expressed the ideas of a Brazilian intelligentsia that was looking toward autonomous economic development. The motives that made Lisboa such a wholehearted follower of Smith's free trade thus becomes clear: his role as a Brazilian author impelled him to it and justified the insistence with which he used Smith to explain the advantages of making Brazil part of the international division of labor.

The same was true in Russia. The most obvious feature of discussion in official spheres in early nineteenth century was the influence of Smith. The official organ of government at that time was *The St. Petersburg Journal,* writers in that newspaper referred to Smith as "a great man, who had seized an important truth". The duty of government should be, according to them, a very easy one. It should not act—for it should only be necessary for it to refrain from interfering. It should only encourage the natural freedom of industry. "Let the government drop all systems of prohibition and control, let it not bind industry by its regulations, and it shall not have to reinforce it by its reward".

Kochubey, the Minister of Interior, apparently impressed with the physiocratic elements of WN. In his report for 1803 speaks of the advisability of leaving private industry free and furnish aid when required. Between 1815 and 1820, free traders of the Imperial Free Economic Society had an organ—*The Spirit of the Journals* (Dukh Jurnalov)—in which they conducted an energetic propaganda for the abolition of protection, translating extracts from the writings of J.B. Say, Bentham, Sismondi and other Western European writers. Free traders were not, however, thorough-going disciples of Smith; they were in a large sense belated physiocrats, insofar as concerned their enthusiasm for agriculture as the sole source of national wealth.

In Spain, liberal economics seeped into colonies through several channels. The Ordinance of 1778, which introduced the policy of *comercio libre*, has sometimes been identified as a free trade measure. It was, of course, nothing of the sort; it merely opened to trade a number of Spanish and American ports which for two and half a centuries had been denied the right to engage in overseas commerce.

Possibly, as Gonzlez Alberdi suggests, WN encouraged some colonialists to press for even greater freedom in their colonial dependence. Few, it would seem, were persuaded to accept all the principles in defense of which Smith and Say wrote so cogently. Much of the credit for making Smith known in Spain belongs to Say, whom some Spaniards called "the French Smith".

If liberal teachers preferred Say for his clarity and simplicity, more radical liberals preferred the books of Bastiat, a most outstanding was *Economic sophisms*. The free trade-protectionism debate did not always run along academic lines and the use of Bastiat's book lowered the theoretical level of the debate. Smith was used as a symbol, but the book read was Bastiat's. Smith was to be a symbol for the free trade supporters and the father of economics for teachers.

WN was not widely read and had few translations if compared with Say and Bastiat. Liberal politicians, more rhetorical than theoretical, preferred Bastiat's arguments to Smith's. Mirabeau, Say and Bastiat were more successful among Spanish economists. I feel this case instructive, perhaps other countries who took Smith for granted as their master of free trade and laissez-faire may reconsider other explanations.

4.4 Lack of Interest in Smithian Theory

Other important issues raised in WN such as education, public debt, capital accumulation, division of labor and so forth (for Smith these are the major "causes of the wealth of nations") received little attention. This leads to observe another interesting phenomenon. In the early stage of spreading WN, it seems that, except for France, most countries were interested in the practical aspects, especially free trade.

Theoretical aspects such as market efficiency, invisible hand theorem and so forth were largely neglected, or considered irrelevant. WN was usually known in fragmentary form, the writers lack the ability to capture the essential analytics; WN was

4 Receptions

referred specifically for practical problems and policies. This is particular so in China as will be explained in the next chapters.

The case of Portugal shows this clearly. Portuguese authors of 1790–1810 did not grasp the analytical structures of mainstream European political economy in the second half of eighteenth century. Laissez-faire were used against the excessive role of state and as a banner for a program of gradual reform of *ancien rgime* institutions. The doctrinaire nature of the assimilation inhibited a clear-cut distinction between the Portuguese authors and the sources that inspired them, insofar as the original messages were filtered for nonscientific purposes.

4.5 Reception By Left-Wing Readers

Let us turn to another aspect: relationship between Smithianism and Marxism in China, Japan and Russia. With the founding of Chinese Communist Party in 1921, Marxism was well received by radical intellectuals. They began to criticize classical economics in the light of Marxist viewpoints. Their criticism gradually gained momentum and continued into the 1930s. Naturally, Smith's ideas became their targets of criticism. WN once again attracted the attention of Chinese academics in the late 1920s, but the first translation (1902) was difficult to read (because Yan Fu used classical style), so Guo and Wang (two Marxists) retranslate WN (published in 1931).

Their motives were unusual: as a preparation for translating *Capital*, they thought WN could be helpful to understand *Capital* better: "The translation of WN was a task entrusted to us by history and we accomplished it before the publication of our version of *Capital*." Both their WN and *Capital* were published in 1931. Neither Guo or Wang did any research on Smith's economics, nor did they comment on it.

It is clear that left-wing readers in China during the 1930s–40s just took Smith's views for criticism without evaluating his social philosophy and economic thought as a whole, and from a historical viewpoint. From the 1950s on, Chinese economists were heavily influenced by the Soviet Union, WN was dismissed as a bourgeois economics or an outdated classical economics, and pigeonholed it. However, considering that classical economics was one of the three sources of Marxism, this second Chinese edition of WN (by Guo and Wang) was reissued in 1972 (Zhu, 1993: 286–9).

A similar phenomenon also existed in Japan, yet with a different flavor. It is common knowledge that in Japan there was and is a strong Marxist tradition of economics in general and of the history of economic thought in particular. Many Japanese specialists on Smith were Marxist sympathizers. There was a trend in which Smith was studied in relation to Marx because Marxism had greatly influenced Japanese social scientists and thinkers since around 1910, and even more so after the post-World War II period.

The Smith–Marx connection in Russia was much more evident. Lenin studied Smith in its original version, which is indicated by citations and references in his works, he also used Russian translations. In many cases he used the analysis of

Smith's ideas found in *Capital*. Lenin characterized Smith as a "great ideologue of the leading bourgeoisie". Lenin's evaluations of Smith is, however, of much greater significance, as it provides the foundation for an objective analysis of the ideology and for the determination of a correct Marxist position in relation to the bourgeois and petty-bourgeois ideologies.

The situation changed after World War II. Evidence of the deep respect for and the interest in the heritage of Smith, on the part of Marxists, became clear at the international scientific conference, organized in 1975 by the Academy of Sciences of the German Democratic Republic and the Martin Luther University in Halle. Soviet scholars had, as early as the 1920s, seriously contributed to Smithian studies.

For the 200th anniversary of Smith's birth, a book by V. M. Stein was published in which the author threw, for the first time, into the scientific forum significant material on Smith that had been published in Western Europe and the USA, in the second half of the nineteenth century and the beginning of the twentieth century. In a somewhat paradoxical manner, Russian Marxists had to defend Smith and the classical school against Populist and nationalist critics.

In the heated discussions of the 1890s, late Russian Populists tried to revive some of Sismondi's teachings, whereas Marxists tried to prove that Smith's and Ricardo's ideas developed by Marx were basically applicable to Russia. In the course of these trilateral ideological confrontations, Lenin coined the basic principle of Russian Marxists toward Smith. Later, Lenin in a way sealed the Russian Marxists' attitude by calling Smith's and Ricardo's political economy the sources of Marxism.

5 Objections

The objection of Smith's free trade and laissez-faire was clear in Russia. Although Catherine II considered Smith's ideas in her *Nakaz* (via Desnitsky's *Proposals*), it appears that her policy needs were of a social and political nature, and very much in line with the traditional Russian Imperial policy. She and her immediate successors were pre-occupied with the issue of serfdom and the maintaining of the autocratic feudal order: there were at least 278 serf rebellions from 1776 to 1798. Russia's environment was not ready for the acceptance of the views of WN. The economic, social and the "humanitarian" objectives of Smith, and those of the Russian government were widely disparate. Even if Catherine was anxious to improve the conditions of peasantry, she was unable to carry her designs into effect, because the whole administrative machinery was in the hands of the class who had power over the peasantry.

A harsh objection came from F. List (1916): *The National System of Political Economy* (Chap. 31). His criticisms are lengthy. To modern readers, these criticisms from a Prussian political economist are not always fair. Here are some excerpts:

> Adam Smith's doctrine is, in respect to national and international conditions, merely a continuation of the physiocratic system. Like the latter, it ignores the very nature of nationalities, seeking entirely to exclude politics and the power of the state... Adam Smith fell into this

kind of fundamental errors in exactly the same way as the physiocrats had done before him, namely, by regarding absolute freedom in international trade as an axiom and by not thoroughly investigating in how far history supported this idea... The mistake has been simply, that this system consists of basically nothing else other than a system of the *private economy of all the individual persons in a country, or of the individuals of the whole human race, as that economy would develop and shape itself, under a state of things in which there were no distinct nations, nationalities, or national interests—no distinctive political constitutions or degree of civilizations—no wars or national animosities* [underlined in original]; that it is nothing more than a theory of value; a mere shopkeeper's or individual merchant's theory— not a scientific doctrine, showing how the productive powers of an entire nation can be called into existence, increased, maintained, and preserved—for the special benefit of its civilization, welfare, might, continuance, and independence. This system regards everything from the shopkeeper's point of view. ... In short, this system is the strictest and most consistent 'mercantile system' ... but if an opinion was needed as to the entire character of a man or of a book, one could not be sufficiently astonished at the narrowness and obliquity of his views.

6 Smith's Impact in Retrospect

One wonders if Smith's impacts were significant in other countries over the past two centuries, evidence above and below seems not supporting this conjecture. In England, when WN was just published in 1776, Sir John Pringle declared "that Dr. Smith, who had never been in trade, could not be expected to write well on that subject any more than a lawyer upon physick" (Boswell: *Life of Samuel Johnson*, Everyman edition, I: 607).

A French magazine *Le journal des sçvants* (February 1777 issue, pp. 81–4) published a notice on WN: "Some of our man of letters who have read it have come to the conclusion that it is not a book that can be translated into our language. They point out, among other reasons, that no one would be willing to bear the expense of publishing because of the uncertain return, and a bookseller least of all. They are bound to admit, however, that the book is full of suggestions and of advice that is useful as well as curious, and might prove of benefit to statesmen" (my translation).

In France, the Italian-born Rossi, Say's successor to the chair of the Collège de France, remarked in the 1840s that the doctrine of economic freedom of Smith was enthusiastically accepted by the French bourgeoisie until they became the rulers of the state, but from then on they seemed to be interested only in protection and in state interference. After the Revolution, Smith had, on the whole, great scientific success but little influence on policies (Palyi, 1928: 217–8).

Smith was recognized as the father of free trade and free economy, the cases of France, Italy and Spain provide evidence that their first ideas of free trade did not come from Smith. The culture language in the Continent until the end of the nineteenth century was French rather than English, the idea of free trade spread within the continent via the works of the physiocrats rather than through WN.

But in other non-European countries such as China and Japan, it was certainly through WN that the ideas of free trade and laissez-faire were transmitted. Smith's impact on policy was limited both across countries and across centuries, his contribution was more at the level of ideas (anti-monopoly, minimal intervention, free market efficiency, etc.), rather than a real-life policy. Ninety years later, my conclusion bears similarity to the observation of Palyi (1928: 180): "the influence of Adam Smith's own idea may have been limited."

Chapter 4
Traduttore Traditore

This Italian expression means "No translation does justice to the original". The best photocopy machine could produce better image than the original but cannot fully reproduce some subtle features of the original piece; the best camera cannot reproduce some nuances of the landscape; and that is why we praise Picasso: he was able to present some striking messages in an abstract form which is very different from the original image.

Similarly, translation is a kind of reconstruction. This is especially true in the case of Yan Fu when China had insufficient knowledge of economics and had inadequate vocabulary and concepts to grasp Smith's messages.

Two ways to defend Yan Fu.

(1) In addition to WN, he also translated other Western books of different disciplines,[1] and it was not an easy task under such conditions. Yan Fu was forced to invent new terms to convey the unfamiliar notions. We should not reproach him for mistranslation; one needs to read with a "sympathetic understanding".
(2) Exact and precise translation is a modern concept. Translation during the sixteenth to nineteenth centuries, in Europe as well as in China, had another connotation and another form of practice: it was not unusual to rewrite/restate in order to facilitate readers. *Traduttore traditore* has no bad meaning, if Yan Fu's translations belong to this style, we should not criticize his simplification, distortion, and rewriting.

With this understanding, this chapter deals with three topics. Section 1 discusses his motivation and how he expected WN be useful. With some examples and modern eyes, Sect. 2 shows how Yan Fu's mistranslation made readers difficult to follow, and some passages were clearly distorted when compared with Smith's text. Section 3 classifies his 310 translator's notes into seven categories (Table 1), explains their features, and how his understandings were diverged from Smith's messages.

---

[1] See Table 1 (Chap. 2) and Schwartz (1964) for an overall evaluation.

1 Motivation of Translation

If Yan Fu's primary concern was in the search of wealth and power, why did he choose a book of 1776 rather than a recent one? Why in 1897 he had an idea to translate a 121-year old book? In the Foreword, he answered in four points. First, one can learn something new from past masters. Second, Smith's criticism of British policies seems useful. Third, past European systems can be served as a good reference for China's reform. Fourth, Smith's book is well written and supported with historical facts.

These four reasons are rather superficial. The question can be restated: How could Yan Fu expect a book like WN, which advocates minimum government and laissez-faire to be useful to China where the public sector was inefficient and the private sector was in disorder around 1900?[2]

Schwartz (1964: 116–7) explained it in two ways. Philosophically, he argued that Smith's individual freedom does not necessarily conflict with the interests of the state. Practically, Schwartz provided a good reason: WN was written in an epoch in which Great Britain dominated the world, so the "wealth and power" of Britain was a living example for China to imitate.

My understandings are different. When Yan Fu was translating WN, Western economics was in a neoclassical era, a leading economist was Alfred Marshall at Cambridge. In his Foreword, Yan Fu mentioned the names of Stanley Jevons, Alfred Marshall, etc., and he was also informed that their method of analysis: using calculus as a new tool with induction and deduction as methods of reasoning. Western economics in the end of the nineteenth century was concerned with what is now termed microeconomics: consumer's surplus, marginal utility analysis, theory of the firm. All these were not useful for China's wealth and power.

What was useful is the political economy analyzed by the classical economists such as Smith and Malthus, in modern words: macroeconomic policy (growth). How can one expect mathematical analysis of microeconomic behavior or Walras's general equilibrium system, which represents neoclassical economics, to help Chinese economy? Yan Fu had absolutely no reason to translate any economics work of neoclassical school that prevailed around 1900s. What was really important, I think, was the title of Smith's book that attracted Yan Fu passionately: *The Wealth of Nations*!

He faced another problem: The dominant mentality prevailed among Chinese intellectuals was pro-agricultural and anti-commercial. This mentality looked down upon affairs related to commerce, the long-run stationary agricultural economy made them deep-rooted physiocrats.

---

[2] Schwartz (1964: 116) expressed this question better as: "Throughout the book we remain constantly aware of the familiar preoccupation with the wealth and power of the state. How, then, is this concern reconcile with Smith's economic individualism? Is not Smith known in the textbooks as the deadly enemy of mercantilism, and is not economic growth for state power almost the heart of mercantilism. ... How can Smith be used for mercantilist purpose?".

A main concern in WN was anti-mercantilism, if the Chinese readers do not understand the background of Smith's doctrines, then Smith's orientation will corresponded perfectly with Chinese anti-commerce mentality. However, one of Yan Fu's purposes was to attack this anti-commerce mentality, so how could he resolve this paradox?

In a Preface to the Chinese version (see Appendix A), Yan Fu's mentor Wu Rulun vividly criticized Chinese intellectuals, saying that they always avoid talking about profits and interests, they are also used to being physiocrats and despising commerce. He then painfully explained the social reasons why the study of economy was not developed in China, and blamed the mandarins for doing nothing: "When the dangerous situation appeared, they could not find useful solutions, but faced the problem helplessly". After that he says: "The book of Adam Smith is a book on interests and profits. He criticized the commercial activities of that epoch, but this does not imply that the translation of this book is to support our anti-commerce tradition. The readers should have this point in mind".

This kind of slogan-like argument could not convince the traditional intellectuals. Yan Fu's defense of WN is clearer and more convincing: Smith's anti-mercantilism argument was because the international commercial activities in England was harmfully corrupted. Like his mentor, he hoped that readers would not use Smith's anti-mercantilism as a support for the traditional anti-commerce mentality. In short, Yan Fu and Wu Rulun tried to explain that Smith's anti-mercantilism should not prevent China from learning the method of "wealth and power" from WN. I doubt if readers were convinced. On the contrary, as will be seen in Sect. 7.2, some important intellectuals disagreed.

Yan Fu provided another argument. At the turn of the twentieth century, the whole of China was impressed by Western technology and opened its arms to welcome everything that was "scientific". He took the advantage of this mentality by presenting WN as a scientific analysis. I have no information to determine if this argument worked.

2 Misunderstanding and Distortion

In his translator's preface to J.S. Mill's *On Liberty*, Yan Fu claimed in 1903 that: "Readers found my translations hard to follow. They do not realize that the original versions are much more difficult. The difficulty lies in the logic and argument, and has nothing to do with the language that I used".

This claim reveals two things. First, readers generally find his texts not easy to understand. Second, he did not (necessarily) grasp the main spirit and the inner logic of the books he translated (covering several disciplines in humanities). Also, his formal education was polytechnic (navy), his taught himself in translating books such as WN.

Let us first examine the terminology appeared in Yan Fu's WN. The 1931 reprinted three-volume version that I used has 978 pages; there are 80 pages of Glossary (about

8% of the total pages) to help readers to understand (or decipher). These 80 pages were added by the publisher, but only of limited help to modern readers.

An important negligence of Yan Fu was that he never put the original names and terms in parentheses so that readers can trace the real meaning or explore further from other references such as encyclopedias and dictionaries. Perhaps he was right in thinking around 1900 that most readers were unable to use Western references.

From the point of view of readers (past and present), his WN is difficult to understand. First, it used terms and names that were unfamiliar to readers. For instance, how can the Western concepts of free trade, point of maximum return be translated into classical Chinese? He did it by using several Chinese characters which sound like to "banke" as the approximate for "bank", without explanation. Readers have to guess the approximate meanings from the context.

Some advanced readers can understand this kind of translation, but how can one understand who F. Quesnay (1694–1774) is, when Yan Fu pronounced this French economist's name in an English way and used three Chinese characters to show this pronunciation, without explaining who Quesnay was? Countless examples like this. Serious readers are obliged to put down the book after every paragraph to think what it means.

Usually, modern readers get lost. In these 80-page glossary I often find entries marked "unidentified", that is, even the annotators in 1931 had difficulties to decipher. Researchers interested in how Yan Fu transformed new foreign terms into classical Chinese (this is another intriguing topic) may explore some instructive messages from this source.

One might argue that despite the inexactness, Smith's main ideas were still conveyed. Yes and No: exact facts were done correctly, but some subtle arguments (such as invisible hand theorem) were lost; more evidence will be discussed in Chap. 5. One is inclined to doubt his understanding about the (complicated) mercantilism debates and the fundamental principles of the classical economics.

Below is a comparison of Smith's text and Yan Fu's translation; this example shows the nature of his style. No further examples are needed to show this aspect, because blaming his translation with modern eyes is unfair and unnecessary. The example is taken from the very beginning page of WN "Introduction and plan of the work", only the first three paragraphs are selected to contrast.

"The annual labour of every nation is the fund which originally supplies it with all the necessaries and conveniences of life which it annually consumes, and which consist always, either in the immediate produce of that labour, or in what is purchased with that produce from other nations".

"According therefore, as this produce, or what is purchased with it, bears a greater or smaller proportion to the number of those who are to consume it, the nation will be better or worse supplied with all the necessaries and conveniences for which it has occasion".

"But this proportion must in every nation be regulated by two different circumstances; first, by the skill, dexterity, and judgment with which its labour is generally applied; and, secondly, by the proportion between the number of those who are employed in useful labour, and that of those who are not so employed. Whatever be the soil, climate, or extent of territory of any particular nation, the abundance or scantiness of its annual supply must, in that particular situation, depend upon those two circumstances" (Smith, 1976: 10).

These three paragraphs are very Smithian style (full of rhetoric skill, recall that Smith was the author of *Lectures on Rhetoric and Belles Lettres*). Let us see how Yan Fu transformed them into one single paragraph. I translated it from an elegant classical style (even more elegant than Smith's text) to show its corresponding contents in plain style.

"All that is needed by a groups of people for living is produced by the labor of its people. The expenses of a nation is supposed to be the same as its national production. When the production exceeds consumption, there is surplus, and with this surplus the people is in comfort situation. On the contrary, it is the deficit that people will be suffered. Four elements determine surplus or deficit: one is skillfulness of labor input; two is the speed of output (production); three is the population involved in production; and four is the profit or deficit of business operation. If the land is considered being distributed fairly but Mr. A has 10 acres and Mr. B has only 5 acres, then we see the differences of their skill. The same is true when Mr. A completed a work in one day and Mr. B in 100 days. Where there are many unemployed people in a country, it is easy to understand why the nation is poor".

It is easy to see how Yan Fu condensed and rewrote Smith's text. If my re-translation is doing justice to Yan Fu's, then Smith was more traduced than translated. I have to say that this is a particular difficult passage that Yan Fu must had hard times: under the constraints of insufficient vocabulary, expression structure in classical Chinese, and the worst is, I am afraid, Yan Fu did not fully understand Smith's subtle messages. The final sentence of my above translation is not stated in Smith's text, it was Yan Fu's invention. This example may show that Yan Fu was doing "more interpretation than translation" or "interpretation through translation".

3 The 310 Translator's Notes

In translating WN Yan Fu added 310 translator's notes, I classified them into seven categories (Table 1). Structurally speaking, Books I, IV and V take up a very large part of his notes (116, 64 and 79 respectively). Taken by categories, most of the notes fall into Categories 2 and 3 (95 and 89 respectively). The length of these notes varied greatly, some have only one line, most of them between half and one page, an extreme example is the note on pages 111-4 (nearly four pages), being longer than Smith's original text.

Some of these notes can be singled out as independent economic propositions. For instance, on pages 339–40 of his translation, irrelevant to Smith's text, he raises the question of whether China should advocate saving (in order to accumulate capital for investment) or advocate consumption (Keynesian type of increasing effective demand). He used nearly two pages to attack this "consumption school". This debates

Table 1 Yan Fu's 310 translator's notes by categories

	Book I	Book II	Book III	Book IV	Book V	Total
(1) Explain that the situation has changes since *WN* was published (1776)	22	5	1	4	1	33
(2) Add new information to supplement the text	34	12	5	25	19	95
(3) Comment on smith's text	33	17	2	24	13	89
(4) Compare Chinese way of thinking with Smith's text	7	0	3	1	5	16
(5) Compare Chinese economy with European economy	2	2	1	2	1	8
(6) Use European examples to show the weakness of China	14	1	0	6	17	38
(7) Present Thorold Rogers' comments on Smith's text	4	2	0	2	23	31
Total	116	39	12	64	79	310

Notes
(1) Chapter 2 Table 1 shows the contents of *WN*
(2) Some notes are hard to classify, for some belonging to two or more categories. In these cases (which are not few), I have assign them to only one category

though independent of Smith's text provides an interesting view of different economic thoughts at that time.

Some of his notes are not classifiable in these seven categories, example: his conception of religion (p. 827). Smith mentioned religion in Chap. 1 of Book V, then in his notes Yan Fu started to compare the religions of China and the West. This is irrelevant to the main text. He sometimes wrote notes to express special ideas.

Another example: "When I read the text, in some places it is so moving that I cannot keep from crying. Alas! how touching Smith's sentences are!" (p. 930). He expressed on many occasions personal feelings, sentiments, unsystematic and impromptu ideas.

Looking over his 310 notes, one realizes his style of notes. First, his analysis of economics was not far away from the "supply and demand" paradigm. Second, with this tool in hand he made some supplements to Smith's text (Categories 2 and 3). He possessed a great deal of general knowledge about China and Europe (Categories 4 and 5). Third, his main concern was the unfavorable situation of China facing foreign penetration, so he used European examples to show the weakness of China (Category 6). In the notes of this Category 6, he frequently added his opinions about state affairs (such as military training).

Objectively speaking, political economy was not his main concern, WN was only one of the books he translated. Yan Fu used some common sense of nineteenth century neoclassical economics to comment on or to criticize Smith's 1776 text. When one reads these notes with modern economics, his notes appeared somewhat elementary, but it is neither fair nor necessary. Below are three examples to show how his notes are matched, diverged or criticized Smith's messages.

(1) *Labor theory of value.* "Labour, therefore, it appears evidently, is the only universal, as well as the only accurate measure of value, or the only standard by which we can compare the values of different commodities at all times and at all places. We cannot estimate, it is allowed, the real value of different commodities from century to century by the quantities of silver which were given for them. We cannot estimate it from year to year by the quantities of corn. By the quantities of labour we can, with the greatest accuracy, estimate it both from century to century and from year to year" (Smith, 1976: 54).

This is a 100% "labour theory of value" prevailed in classical economics until Marx. With the late nineteenth-century neoclassical economics knowledge, Yan Fu criticized this proposition (page 26–7 note): "Smith used the labour force involved in the commodity to determine its real value and had allowed the differences of labor qualities in his considerations, but even the wisest man sometimes nods. There is no such a thing as fixed value for a product, it depends purely on the interaction of demand and supply: if the supply was less than the demand, and if it was hard to acquire, the price is dear; and vice versa. ... An acre of land located in a remote place is hard to sale for several ounces of gold, but it will become a ten-thousand ounces gold object if it was located in the city. Has this anything to do with labor force input? ... And that is why later economists did not follow Smith's value theory of labor."

This is an excellent note in which he explains Smith basic ideas, its illogic reasoning, offered a counter-example, and why later economists were departed from this theory. I find only a similar note of this kind in the end of Chap. 11 of Book I, as will be analyzed in detail in Sect. 5.2 ("1 On rent theory").

(2) *Determinants of wages.* "Secondly, the wages of labour do not in Great Britain fluctuate with the price of provisions. These vary every-where from year to year, frequently from month to month. But in many places the money price of labour remains uniformly the same sometimes for half a century together. ... The high price of provisions during these ten years past has not in many parts of the kingdom been accompanied with any sensible rise in the money price of labour. It has, indeed, in some; owing probably more to the increase of the demand for labour, than to that of the price of provisions. Thirdly, as the price of provisions varies more from year to year than the wages of labour, so, on the other hand, the wages of labour vary more from place to place than the price of provisions. ..." (Smith, 1976: 92).

Smith explains the situation between wages and provisions in the UK, saying that there is no simple single rule to explain it. In a short note (page 79) Yan Fu commented: "It is a general principle that wage rate does not fluctuate with food, and it is not only so in the UK. However, most mercantilists doubt about this principle. I think that is because they do not understand that price fluctuations are totally depended on the interaction between supply and demand. It is often heard that it was because the low price of food in China that made Chinese wages low, I think this saying shares the same misunderstanding of the mercantilists".

Let me interpret this note from modern eyes. During the eighteenth century, UK was started to be industrialized, labor supply was not "unlimited" as often observed in pre-industrial societies and in today's developing economies. In the case of UK, when labor supply is limited, market wages are normally higher than subsistence wages, i.e., higher than price of provisions: if food price changes, wages will be increase either proportionally or higher. While around 1900s, China was an "unlimited labor supply economy" in which supply of labor exceeded the demand; theoretically the market wages were equal or lower than the subsistence level, hence sensibly affected by the price of provisions. Yan Fu used a simple supply–demand concept to criticize British mercantilists and general opinions in China without discriminating the basic structure difference in both economies; this invalidates his criticism.

(3) *Unequal exchange.* "Every town draws its whole subsistence, and all the materials of its industry, from the country. It pays for these chiefly in two ways: first, by sending back to the country a part of those materials wrought up and manufactured; ... secondly, by sending to it a part of both of the rude and manufactured produce, either of other countries, or of distant parts of the same country, imported into the town;... They give the traders and artificers in the town an advantage over landlords, farmers, and labourers in the country, and breakdown that natural equality which would otherwise take place in the commerce which is carried on between them. ... By means of those regulations a greater share of it is given to the inhabitants of the town that would otherwise fall to them; and a less to those of the country" (Smith, 1976: 141–2).

This clearly explains the unequal exchange mechanism between town and country. Using a modern terminology prevailed in the 1970s, it is the dependency of the country on the town that made the "core" exploit the "periphery". In his note (page 144–5) Yan Fu applied this principle to the relationship between China and Western powers: "There is no manufactured goods exported from China to foreign countries, and few goods from abroad are raw materials. So the relationship between China and foreign countries is similar to the relationship between country and town, and between agriculture and industry. What Smith said, when changed to another place with another name, is suitable to describe the commercial situation between China and foreign countries. ...". Both Smith and Yan Fu fully understood the argument of modern dependency theory.

Chapter 5
Yan Fu's Understanding of *The Wealth of Nations*

Yan Fu's 310 notes provide rich information for the following analysis. (1) Did he understand Smith's text correctly, or did he follow well Smith's arguments? (2) What kind of criticisms had Yan Fu made toward Smith's ideas? (3) How he praised Smith's economics?

Under space constraint, I select interesting passages (about half) from my Chinese text. It is rewarding to read his elegant (and difficult) style in the original text that no translation can convey its flavor. I use Yan Fu:123 to indicate his translator's note in page 123 of the Chinese version (pocket-size edition); and Smith 1976:456 to indicate page 456 of the Glasgow edition of WN published by Oxford University Press in 1976. All Yan Fu's notes are my translation, a kind of sentence by sentence restatement.

1 General Economic Arguments

1.1 Pasture Yields As Good a Rent As Corn Land, and Sometimes a Greater One

> In some particular local situations it is quite otherwise, and the rent and profit of grass are much superior to what can be made by corn. (Smith, 1976: 165) Yan Fu's comment (p. 177): There are two reasons to explain why rent of grass land is superior to rice (corn) land: one is population growth that increased the demand for meat, that made cattle and sheep dearer, hence higher profit; two is because the costs to raise animals are lower than corn production, so the required capital is lower.

His comments may sustain, I would like to offer another explanation: The superiority of British wool industry in the world market induced more and more corn land transformed to grass land that was a well-known story of "enclosure movement." The demand of land for corn reduced because foreign corn was cheaper; it was a kind of specialization in the international production. In Smith's time, this reason may be more important than Yan Fu's first point.

His second point (lower costs and lower investment) is discussible. His implicit reasoning run like this: Lower costs and higher price means higher profit margin, which means higher productivity, and according to Ricardo's differential rent theory, one pays higher rent. It was quite possible that Yan Fu had this theory in mind in 1902, but overall I think higher profitability of wool over corn that caused higher demand of land for grass is a more general explanation than Yan Fu's.

1.2 On the Determination of the Value of Gold and Silver

> The discovery of the new [precious metal] mines, however, as the old ones come to be gradually exhausted, is a matter of the greatest uncertainty, and such as no human skill or industry can ensure. All indications, it is acknowledged, are doubtful, and the actual discovery and successful working of a new mine can alone ascertain the reality of its value, or even of its existence. ... Its nominal value, the quantity of gold and silver by which this annual produce could be expressed or represented, would, no doubt, be very different; ...the cheapness and abundance of gold and silver plate, would be the sole advantage which the world could derive from the one event, and the dearness and scarcity of those trifling superfluities the only inconveniency it could suffer from the other. (Smith, 1976: 254–5)

The background for Smith's passage was that since the fifteenth century precious metals flowed into Europe from Latin America, caused the so-called price revolution. These metals propelled international trade, but in the long-run, European countries began to realize that metals are not equal to real wealth: More gold and silver do not mean more real purchasing power and realized that "money as a veil" or "money illusion."

Yan Fu commented this idea in three notes (pp. 202–3, 215–6, 254–5). First, "Even a nation possesses abundant gold, it does not imply that nation is wealthy, the reason is quite evident. Most people confined by common knowledge do not realize this phenomenon. Precious metals are nothing but a standard of exchange, their function is something like chips in the gambling: when more chips available, they represent less value, and vice versa; they have only nominal, not real value. If a nation was not aiming to increase the production of goods but only intended to accumulate gold, silver, pearls etc., this is just like a gambler who see chips are valuable today, and expect that will be more valuable tomorrow, so he aims to accumulate chips continuously. He does not realize that when chips become abundant, the value they represent will be less and less. The real wealth of a gambler is not represented by chips, just like a nation's wealth is not measured by silver and gold. Without this insight, traders are striving for silver balance, not commodity stock; people are envied when hearing new gold and silver mines were discovered, but senseless when hearing new coal or iron mines were explored. ..." (pp. 202–3).

This idea is correct for European countries where silver and gold are abundant. This is something like to tell people in a wealth country that more food does not imply more health. To people in a starving country, the question is not excessive but scarce. If European countries during the sixteenth–eighteenth centuries were charitable to donate excessive precious metals to a silver famine country like China, although the real wealth of China would not be increased thereby, but certainly will not think these metals are harmful.

Yan Fu had a good explanation. "The value of gold and silver is, as in the case of commodity, determined by supply and demand, not by their quantities. The quantity of platinum is less than gold but its price is cheaper than gold; many chemical elements are difficult to extract or hard to find, but their prices are not high, so the quantity is not the sole determinant of value. When a country has no mines of precious metals and relies on imports, the value of silver and gold are determined by the value of commodities exchanged; they are primarily determined by the law of supply and demand" (pp. 215–6).

Smith's money illusion explanation is valid in a macroeconomic framework when demand is satisfied and supply is handily available. In China where demand for silver was so strong in most times and most supply of silver depended on foreign supply, under this "more demand than supply" situation, the value of precious metals should not be an "illusion" as in European countries.

Why Yan Fu agreed with Smith's idea and thinking that idea is applicable to China? "Smith's view on the value of gold and silver was an outstanding insight. Europeans viewed gold and silver as measures of wealth, they were awaken after realized Smith's insight" (pp. 256–7). I have two comments: (1) Why European had the view of "metals equal wealth" (like Chinese) prior to the seventeenth century? It was because the demand for metals was greater than supply (like China). But the situation changed in Smith's time: The relationship between supply and demand was inverted. (2) Smith was certainly not a first to offer the idea of money illusion; Thomas Mun and David Hume before him already pronounced it.

It is paradoxical to read Yan Fu's another passage on the value of silver in China: "Recently silver value in China is quite low, lost about one-third of its value compared to three decades ago. Silver that we have accumulated so hardly became a source of deficits, the wealth of our nation was reduced owing to international silver slump, and this loss is certainly not a small one! Not a minor one!" (p. 257).

The background for this observation was this. Since the 1870s the gold standard has replaced the silver/gold bimetallism that prevailed over the past centuries, silver was thus no longer an international exchange standard. There was an oversupply of silver, the consequence was a serious price drop. Silver countries like India, China and Japan were damaged, that is why Yan Fu was so sad about silver value.

If he was so sensible about silver value, then how can we understand his previous notes that agreed with Smith's idea "silver and gold do not equal to national wealth"? And how to understand his metaphor that silver and gold are nothing but like gambler's chips that do not represent real wealth? The paradox is evident.

My metaphor for this paradox is food calories: For food abundant and cheap country like the USA, more calories does not mean better health. But in starved countries, calories are lifesaver. On a theoretical side, Yan Fu agreed with Smith's ideas but on a practical side, this idea was not applicable to China. Yan Fu's comments are conflicting.

1.3 Interest Rates and Precious Metals

> Mr. Locke, Mr. Law, and Mr. Montesquieu, as well as many other writers, seem to have imagined that the increase of the quantity of gold and silver, in consequence of the discovery of the Spanish West Indies, was the real cause of the lowering of the rate of interest through the greater part of Europe. Those metals, they say, having become of less value themselves, the use of any particular portion of them necessarily became of less value too, and consequently the price which could be paid for it. This notion, which at first sight seems so plausible, has been fully exposed by Mr. Hume, that it is, perhaps, unnecessary to say anything more about it. (Smith, 1976: 353–4)

Smith did not explain briefly Hume's ideas in WN, and this unexplained argument puzzled many later readers who are not familiar with the whole issue: other things being equal, when monetary supply increased, interest rate lowered; and vice versa. This is a simple mechanism anybody would agree, but why Smith and Hume disagreed?

Yan Fu also puzzled (page 354 of his note): "interest rate was paid by silver and gold [i.e. depend on metals], I do not understand why the view hold by Locke and others was wrong, later scholars should correct this argument." He thought that Locke's opinion is a common sense and did not understand why Smith agreed with Hume's idea.

That is because Locke and Yan Fu had quantity theory of money in mind, that interest rate has an inverse relationship with quantity of money. To help readers, the editors of the Glasgow edition compares all these gentlemen's points in a lengthy footnote (p. 353, note 9); it is sufficient to quote Hume's point (p. 354 note 10) to show why Smith agreed.

> David Hume 'Of interest', *Essays Moral, Political, and Literary,* ed. Green and Grose, i.321: 'Price have risen near four times since the discovery of the INDIES; and it is probable gold and silver have multiplied much more: But interest has not fallen much above half. The rate of interest, therefore, is not derived from the quantity of the precious metals.' And more positively, 'High interest arise from *three* circumstances: A great demand for borrowing; little riches to supply that demand; and great profits arising from commerce: And these circumstances are a clear proof of the small advance of commerce and industry, not of the scarcity of gold and silver.' (Ibid., 322) (Smith, 1976: 354)

This is a convincing argument, both supply/demand and the particular feature of the economy were considered. Yan Fu would have agreed if equipped with is background.

1.4 The Fall in the Price of Corn Since the Establishment of the Bounty is Due to Other Causes

> The average price of corn, it has been said, has fallen considerably since the establishment of the bounty. That the average price of corn began to fall somewhat towards the end of the last century, and has continued to do so during the course of the sixty-four first years of the present, I have already endeavoured to show. But this event, supposing it to be as real as I believe it to be, must have happened in spite of the bounty, and cannot possibly have happened in consequence of it. ... This gradual fall in the average price of grain, it is probable, therefore, is ultimately owing neither to the one regulation nor to the other, but to that gradual and insensible rise in the real value of silver, ... It seems to be altogether impossible that the bounty could ever contribute to lower the price of grain. (Smith, 1976: 506–7)

The Glasgow edition prepared several notes (pp. 506–7) to explain the background of this issue happened in England and France. Yan Fu's comments deserve discussion: "Smith thought low corn price in England during the eighteenth century was caused by higher price of silver, later economists doubt about this explanation because by that time the quantity of silver flowed into Europe was not less, countries began to use more gold; silver price in France was even cheaper, so there is no reason for silver price to rise. I think the low price of corn was mainly due to the improvement of agricultural technique and more lands were explored. Farmers knew better about rotation system and with new crops to explore land fertility. The new land system, new know-how about grass, and the advertisements of seeds as one can see in the newspapers of that time, all showed the advancement of agriculture productivity. Moreover, the weather was also favorable so that we see the rapid population growth in England: by the end of the seventeenth century in the south of England the population was about five millions, it doubled to nearly ten millions by the mid-eighteenth century. And that is not all, in addition to low corn price, rent became higher so that landlord are much richer. Taken together, lower corn price, higher rent, doubled population etc. are signs of economic development, not simply caused by the value of silver. ..." (pp. 490–1).

Theoretically, this multi-sector causality arguments were superior to Smith's single-factor explanation. As to the effect of bounty on corn price, Yan Fu said nothing about it. The 1976 Glasgow edition provides a related information: "In commenting on Smith's critique of the bounty, Pownall remarked (*Letter*, 31–7) on the similarity between Smith and Necker, and suggested that Smith had copied the latter's 'decisive proof' that the bounty on corn had not lowered prices. Necker's proof was that a general fall in the price of corn had taken place in France despite a prohibition on its export." (Smith, 1976: 507, Footnote 8)

1.5 On Mercantilism

After translated Book IV Chap. 8 "Conclusion of the Mercantile System," he wrote: "What Smith criticized [regarding the defects of mercantilism system] in this chapter were all abolished within decades. It was partly due to Smith's book, also due to the businessmen of that time who realized that the regulatory mercantile system was disadvantageous, hindered the development of trade. All these factors made the reform possible and easy. A good reader may learn plenty of economics principles from this chapter, one see not only the views hold by policy makers and businessmen in England a century ago, but also see how the old mercantile system was harmful to national economy. It is also evident when people were in search of self-interest, the result will be in conflict with the real interest [of the whole society]. What I do not understand is why people in England were so late to realize these drawbacks and revolted the system. Reading Smith's book today [around 1900], I have seen the regulatory system in England abolished and that free trade prevailed. However, recently people in the United States are still held the view for inner-development [i.e. close-door policy], it is hard to understandable that even the Americans were fully aware of the historical lessons in England, but still follow the wrong track. My opinion is that Americans were so deeply rooted in their own system, and they are ignorant about the management of the economy. What is certain is their orientation will be harmful to the nation [America], and the results will be more seriously than before [in England]. If so, they will also be more difficult to disentangle from the situation than before [in England]" (p. 660).

My comments. (1) Yan Fu was a naïve liberalism, taking it as a truth beyond time and place. He considered free trade and laissez-faire policies are all good for any country at every stage of development; liberalism is unconditionally superior to mercantilism and protectionism. (2) It seems that he was not aware that free trade policy in England did not last long (see Irwin, 2015 for a comprehensive study). (3) Economic conditions varied from nation to nation. Even for the same country, its international competitivity varied from time to time. When England was dominant in Smith's time, free trade was a favorable policy; but no more so today. (4) Yan Fu admired liberalism that helped British power and thought this may be applicable to every country as an effective policy. We know now that there is no such panacea.

2 Criticisms on Smith's Doctrines

2.1 Theories of Rent

After completed Book I Chap. 9 "Of the Profits of Stock," Yan Fu wrote a 4-page note (pp. 111–4), this is the longest one among his 310 notes. It contains various topics including profit, wage, population, etc., I shall confined to his main subject (theories of rent) to show (1) how he offered Ricardo's rent theory to contrast with that of Smith's; (2) how he was puzzled by the differences between the two views; (3) how he summarized James Mill's "Rent" to add further doctrine of rent theory; (4) He was confused by different theories, his summaries also confused readers.

"Ricardo says: when the population growth approaches its limit, wage rate and profit rate also decrease, only land rent will increase because fertile lands became exhausted and bad lands were explored. When the population of a nation grows and the available capital also increased, rich people still willing to invest despite the decreasing profit rate. ... The more population is, the more bad lands are explored; since the output of each land is different, so is the rent for each land, and that is why rent for fertile lands increased. (The productivity of a land depend on its fertility, and if its location is convenience for transportation)" (pp. 111–2).

What he presented here is the famous Ricardian differential rent theory that appeared in the early nineteenth century, decades after Smith's death. David Ricardo (1772–1823) says that the difference of rent between two pieces of land is due to their productivity differences. Suppose there are ten categories of land A, B, C, ..., J, people will use category A land first and gradually move to D and E categories.

When the worse lands (G, H) are exploited, rent of better lands (A, B) will be increased "automatically," as the productivity differences between A, B and G, H are widened. We name this notion as Ricardo's "differential rent." What Yan Fu said above was in this Ricardian spirit.

Why present Ricardo's theory when translating Smith? Because when translating WN, he found the rent theory he heard (the nineteenth century Ricardian version) was quite different from Smith wrote in WN (eighteenth century rent theory). He was confused but unable to offer a contrasting explanation.

To further complicate the problem, he presented counter-arguments hold by French economists (such as Turgot) vis-à-vis Ricardo's theory: "Later economists criticized Smith that although he was a founder of political economy but there are defects in his doctrines, some shallow economists discarded Smith's ideas perfunctorily. The profoundness of Smith's doctrine is often neglected by readers, and that is why although there are revisions of Smith's doctrines but few are superior. In fact, land rent is determined by two factors: one is the quantity of population, the other is the sophistication of agriculture technique. When population is scarce and corn price is low, farmer's income can only meet the needs for living; in this case no rent is possible even if the land is fertile, this explains how population affected rent. If the agriculture technique was underdeveloped and lands were not carefully utilized, in this case no rent is possible even if the land is fertile and corn price is high; this explains the importance of agriculture technique. The growth of population therefore depends on both fertile land and sophisticated technique. If we see from this perspective, then the Ricardian reasoning reversed the logic of reasoning: it was the population growth that pushed farmers from good lands [A, B] to bad lands [I, J], and this is not a convincing theory. The following historical evidence from England supported Smith's theory: the rent of an acre of land in the suburban was six pence centuries ago, is now more than 120 times dearer, but the output increased only about nine times. This enormous difference is mainly due to population growth, and certainly cannot be explained by Ricardo's theory that it was because worse lands were exploited. Another factor is, as said above, the progress of agriculture technique. Ricardo's theory is therefore neither original nor convincing" (pp. 167–8).

This is a meaningful counter-argument: population growth, technical progress and other factors made rent differences in real world did not work as Ricardo's theory predicted. So shall we listen to Ricardo or to Smith? Both. Historians of economic theory know that Ricardo's differential rent theory was invented for another purpose: to determine the shares of national income, to be distributed to workers, landlord and capitalists. Let me briefly explain his framework.

According Malthusian "iron wage" doctrine, workers' wage rate in the long-run will be equal to the subsistence level: if he earns more, he will produce more children and that will consume more than what he earned and vice versa. So, it is reasonable (in their view) to assume that in the long-run a worker's wage is equal to his subsistence level.

If we know the average wage rate and the total number of workers in a society, we know easily how much of the national income will go to the working class (suppose 30%). But we do not know how landlords and capitalists will share the rest (70%), and that is the place Ricardo's theory will be useful.

Suppose there are ten categories of land in a society, and suppose we know: (1) the productivity difference of each category and (2) total acreage of each category. Then by Ricardo's differential rent theory, we can "theoretically" add up all rent income for all categories of land (i.e., to aggregate the difference of rent between categories A, B to I, J, and multiplied by total acreage of each category). By doing so, we know the total income of the landlord class (suppose 45%). The rest of national income (25%), by definition, goes to the capitalists.

Ricardo's differential rent theory was designed for such a particular purpose. It cannot, of course, be used to predict which land will generate how much rent and the fluctuation of rent of that land over the past centuries. Ricardo's theory of rent is a macroeconomic device to determine national income distribution (i.e., how GDP is distributed among classes). While Smith's rent theory is a microeconomic point of view: rent is determined by demand and supply, by the costs invested in the land, by its location and by its productivity, etc.

In other words, there is no single clear-cut factor that determines rent in Smith's perspective: even institutional constraint matters. Yan Fu did not explain this background, but he was honest enough to present conflicting theories. His readers who knew so little about political economy around the 1900s must also be confused.

Some 20 pages later in another note (pp. 194–5) Yan Fu asked himself: if Ricardo's theory is objectionable, why so many economists followed? He repeated Smith's basic idea, Ricardo's basic point, and some counter-arguments against Ricardo, but still puzzled. He concluded: "However, Ricardo's theory must have some truth that cannot be objected, and that is what scholars should be investigated carefully" (p. 195).

This is not the end of his confusion. When completed Book I Chap. 11 "Of the Rent of Land," he wrote a note to conclude: "This chapter on land is the longest (heaviest) one in WN, there are some elegant passages but also some defects about the causes of rent. ... We find no consistent principle in Smith's rent theory, in

2 Criticisms on Smith's Doctrines

many cases we see his isolated examples, and after several paragraphs we see his explanations conflicting each other, ... there are some profound insights but we also see his fragmentary explanations that does not make a consistent principle. I hope later economists can make up this deficiency from two aspects. First, to explain the nature of rent, why and how it is different from other economic goods? Second, what are the causes of rent fluctuation?" (p. 271).

This revealed his sources of confusion, although both questions are well posed, to which economists in the 1900s already have good answers to offer. Yan Fu was not aware of all these. He was neither satisfied with Smith's theory nor convinced by Ricardo's, so how he explain readers which theory is better? He found a way to escape from this trouble: to translate a currently prevailing theory of rent.

"... Although Ricardo's theory is still criticized by German and American economists, but later economists such as Walker, Marshall also defended Ricardo's theory, so I know his theory should not be abandoned. Given this is an important theory, what I can do is to translate James Mill's writing on rent as an appendix to this chapter. ..." (p. 271). For this, he spent five pages (pp. 272–6) to summarize Mill (1821): *Elements of Political Economy*, Chap. 2, Sect. 1 "Rent." Mill's text contains 11 pages, I find Yan Fu summarized and rewrote Mill's messages more or less correctly. This ended his long struggle with theories of rent, but the battlefield is still messy.

2.2 Law of Supply and Demand

> The dearness of house-rent in London arise, not only from those causes which render it dear in all great capitals, the dearness of labour, the dearness of all the materials of building, which must generally be brought from a great distance, and above all the dearness of ground-rent, every landlord acting the part of a monopolist, ... but it arises in part from the peculiar manners and customs of the people, which oblige every master of a family to hire a whole house from top to bottom. (Smith, 1976: 134)

Yan Fu commented: "high rent level in cities is caused by more demand than supply. The three reasons that Smith said [dearness of labour, materials of building and ground-rent] are all true factors but people in London still willing to pay high rent. Smith explained high rent with these three reasons, was actually a fallacious explanation that readers should be bear in mind" (p. 134).

I disagree with his comment and in favor of Smith's. Yan Fu's criticism is that Smith explained only from the cost side and neglected the supply/demand side. If Smith said nothing about this, it was not Smith unaware of it but he wanted to emphasize another more important factor (the institutional constraint): "...the peculiar manners and customs of the people, which oblige every master of a family to hire a whole house from top to bottom."

In several notes Yan Fu revealed his firm conviction of supply/demand law, and criticized that Smith did not obey it. An example is in Smith 1976:183 where he explained the price of coal is kept down by that of wood, which varies with the state of agriculture. This is a reasonable explanation but Yan Fu disagreed strongly: "In many occasions Smith did not followed supply/demand law closely and that is why he was often criticized by later scholars. ... Once a law is established, it is inappropriate to apply it to certain cases and also claim that same law cannot be applied elsewhere. If so, the law cannot be sustained" (p. 195). Yan Fu took the supply/demand "law" (conditional true) as if a physics "law" (universally true): there is no such a law in social sciences.

2.3 Corn as Standard of Value

> Upon all these accounts, therefore, we may rest assured, that equal quantities of corn will, in every state of society, in every stage of improvement, more nearly represent, or be equivalent to, equal quantity of labour, than equal quantity of any other part of the rude produce of land. Corn, accordingly, it has already been observed, is, in all different stages of wealth and improvement, a more accurate measure of value than any other commodity or set of commodities. In all those different stages, therefore, we can judge better of the real value of silver, comparing it with corn, than by comparing it with any other commodity, or set of commodities. (Smith, 1976: 206)

The message is clear: value of silver in Europe changed so frequently that Smith thought it was not a good long-run standard of value. On the other hand, over a long period, the labor input for an output of 1000 kg of corn remain nearly the same in his times, so from the viewpoint of labor theory of value, Smith thought it is safer to use corn as a standard of value.

Yan Fu objected (note p. 214): (1) Land fertility varies from place to place, the required labor input for every acre is differed. (2) Agriculture technique improved so quickly that the same quantity of land and labor today are much more productive than yesterday. (3) Land production is constrained by the "law of diminishing return" and "point of maximum return." He argues that corn is visibly not a good standard of value. He repeated similar view in another note (page 255).

Searching for invariant standard of value was a concern of classical economists, especially David Ricardo. What Yan Fu said are not new to Smith, he was overreacted to Smith's message. What Smith tried to argue is that, as a standard of value, corn is better than precious metals; he never says that corn is an "absolute" standard of value.

Yan Fu's reaction was: land productivity varied so greatly from place to place and from time to time, using corn as a standard is against common sense. The difference is: Smith had a "relative" idea, while Yan Fu had an "absolute" standard in mind. Even today in many developing countries where famine exist or where inflation rates are high, the value of corn could be more stable than metals. Smith's idea is not totally wrong.

2.4 Navigation Acts

> The Act of Navigation is not favourable to foreign commerce, or to the growth of that opulence which can arise from it. ... As defence, however, is of much more importance than opulence, the act of navigation is, perhaps, the wisest of all the commercial regulations of England. (Smith, 1976: 464–5)

Yan Fu was quite upset to read Smith, hero of economic liberalism, to praise this kind of interventionist policy. On page 460, he strongly criticized Smith that this idea is a self-destruction of the laissez-passer spirit. But he also tried to defend Smith that the prevailing opinion in Smith's time favored this Act, such that Smith was not intend to against the public.

A second thought urged him to say that the historical evidence do not support the necessity of this Act; he finally condemned Smith for "writing inappropriate arguments to favor the Act." Yan Fu was an "absolutist" as we have seen his fixed idea on the "law" of supply and demand; he also suggested applying British liberalism to America.

Here, we see his absolute view of liberalism to England, and we shall see later his proposal of unconditional liberalism for Chinese economy. In fact, Smith was simply practical: he advocated economic liberalism when it does more benefits than harms to England, but when national defense is "much more importance than opulence," his liberalism retreats.

2.5 Meaningless Passages

> The soldiers of a standing army, though they may never have seen an enemy, yet have frequently appeared to possess all the courage of veteran troops, and the very moment that they took the field to have been fit to face the hardiest and most experienced veterans. In 1756, when the Russian army marched into Poland, the valour of the Russian soldiers did not appear inferior to that of Prussians, ... (Smith, 1976: 705)

What Yan Fu had in mind was to learn "the nature and causes" from WN for China. It is understandable that he was not interested in this kind of military story, and showed his impatience: "What Smith said in this section is not interesting and convincing, readers only need to know Smith also wrote this kind of things in WN" (p. 701).

Yan Fu also deleted some parts: "Digression concerning Bank of deposit, particularly that of Amsterdam" (Book IV.iii.b), and lengthy paragraphs in Book V.i.f "Article 2d. Of the expense of the Institutions for the Education of Youth," for instance: "It was not so with that either of the Greek, or of the Hebrew language. The Infallible decrees of the church had pronounced the Latin translation of the Bible, ..." (Smith, 1976: 766). He thought these are irrelevant to his readers, and this also explains why only about 60% of WN were translated.

3 Praises for Smith's Analyses

3.1 Basic Attitude

In his Foreword, Yan Fu says: "Truth is not generated only by debates, it must also be evident from facts. Copernicus's doctrine is now fully accepted and no one can reject it; his theory is true when we project millions of years backward, and it will still be true million years hence. We should not doubt the principles contained in Smith's book; we will benefit if we follow his principles, and will be damaged if we do not." (p. 4). This is another evidence of his absolutism: to compare Smith's economics to Copernicus's astronomy laws. This kind of unconditional acceptance, despite some criticisms discussed above, seems passionately naïve.

3.2 Anti-bullionism

> But we should remember, that the more gold we import from one country, the less we must necessarily import from all others. The effectual demand for gold, like that for every other commodity, is in every country limited to a certain quantity. If nine-tenths of this quantity are imported from one country, there remain a tenth only to be imported from all others. The more gold besides that is annually imported from some particular countries, over and above what is requisite for plate and for coin, the more must necessarily be exported to some others; and the more, that most insignificant object of modern policy, the balance of trade, appears to be in our favour with some particular countries, the more it must necessarily appear to be against us with many others. (Smith, 1976: 548–9)

This is a typical anti-bullionism argument: the wealth of a nation is not measured by the quantity of metals; accumulating metals through trade balance will push the domestic price higher and weaken her competitivity abroad. The final result is that country will buy foreign cheaper products with previously accumulated metals that will be reversibly out-flowed. Yan Fu's note reads: "This is the most profound insight in Smith's economics, later scholars can hardly add or revise this principle. It is really remarkable that Smith could have such an insight at that time, and this qualifies him as the founder of this discipline" (p. 537). In fact, this is David Hume's well-known price-specie flow mechanism; Yan Fu over-praised Smith.

3.3 On Monopoly

> But since the fall of the power of Portugal, no European nation has claimed the exclusive right of sailing in the Indian seas, of which the principal ports are now open to the ships of all European nations. Except in Portugal, however, and within these few years in France, the trade to the East Indies has in every European country been subjected to an exclusive company. Monopolies of this kind are properly established against the very nation which

erects them. The greater part of that nation are thereby not only excluded from a trade to which it might be convenient for them to turn some part of their stock, but are obliged to buy the goods which that trade deals in, somewhat dearer than if it was open and free to all their countrymen. Since the establishment of the English East India company, for example, the other inhabitants of England, over and above being excluded from the trade, must have paid in the price of the East India goods which they have consumed, not only for all the extraordinary profits which the company may have made upon these goods in consequence of their monopoly, but for all the extraordinary waste which the fraud and abuse, inseparable from the management of the affairs of so great a company, must necessarily have occasioned. The absurdity of this second kind of monopoly, therefore, is much more manifest than that of the first. (Smith, 1976: 631)

This is a beautiful passage that explains major shortcomings of mercantilism that Smith attacked, to which he proposed liberalism (free trade). In a one-page length note (p. 627) Yan Fu explained a brief history of East India Companies of England and Holland, the troubles thereby caused and the expensive costs in the fighting for monopolies. He concluded by praising: "All these evidence supports that what Smith said was true. People in England thought that since the establishment of East India Company, the nation's wealth was seriously harmed; and its wealth effect to the civil was also limited. If this company was well managed with correct strategy, it should have done great fortune to England. Smith was living in the seventeenth [*sic*, 18th] century, had so sharp insights about national economy, was truly an extraordinary great man" (p. 627). Again, this is an over-praise because this kind of ideas was prevailed before the mid-eighteenth century.

3.4 Some Defects

WN contains some insightful concepts, such as "invisible hand theorem," "diamond-water paradox," "the division of labor is limited by the extent of the market." Did Yan Fu transmitted these concepts effectively? No, because what he had in mind was to learn useful policies from the powerful British Empire, pure academic and logic issues were not his concerns. Most passages related to theoretical issues were omitted or "mis-translated." Here is a telling example.

As every individual, therefore, endeavours as he can both to employ his capital in the support of domestick industry, and so to direct that industry that its produce may be of the greatest value; every individual necessarily labours to render the annual revenue of the society as great as he can. He generally, indeed, neither intends to promote the publick interest, nor knows how much he is promoting it. By preferring the support of domestick to that of foreign industry, he intends only his own security; and by directing that industry in such a manner as its produce may be of the greatest value, he intends only his own gain, and he is in this, as in many other cases, led by an invisible hand to promote an end which was no part of it. …. (Smith, 1976: 456)

Yan Fu's translation of this famous passage reads: "It is not because they know what they are doing fits the benefits of the public or will be beneficial to the country; their purpose was to prevent any loss of their own fortune. They are engaged in more profitable business and avoided meager profit business. What they are doing are based on self-interest motivation; even if the State has done nothing, the whole nation was thereby benefited. The benefits of a nation will not be damaged by these self-interest activities; only when the citizen pursuit their self-interest and the nation is thereby benefited, the interest of the nation is realized" (p. 449).

The point here is he omitted the most crucial keywords: "led by an invisible hand to promote an end which was no part of it." If someone argues that although his translation was not faithful, he might be quite followed Smith's spirit. Let me answer this by a sentence in his another note (p. 660, cited earlier in Sect. 1 "5 On mercantilism"): "it is also evident when people were in search of self-interest, the result will be in conflict with the real interest [of the whole society]."

If he really understood the invisible hand theorem, with his Confucian education and having China's situation in mind, he would not have agreed. I am not intend to expose his mistranslation or distortion; we have to be sympathetic to his endeavor, although his understanding of WN and criticism of Smith are sometimes discussible.

Chapter 6
Yan Fu's Economic Ideas

In some of his 310 translator's notes, Yan Fu expressed his own comments. They are not systematic arguments, in many occasions, he expressed feelings, sentiments and impromptu ideas. His ideas are not mature enough to be named "thought," but the contents are rich enough to answer the following issues.

(1) What were the major problems of Chinese economy in his eyes? (2) How he understood and responded to Smith's liberalism? (3) What he said on some Chinese economic issues? (4) His background was navy academy, what were the major sources he based to argue?

Literature on Yan Fu is abundant (mostly in Chinese language), but few economists were engaged in this topic. The published ones such as Luo (1978) and Shi (1978) are either too brief or too general to be instructive.

A comprehensive one is Hou and Wu (1983), in 60 pages they discussed Yan Fu's economic ideas in detail. A major difference is: they analyzed Yan Fu's materials basically from a Marxist perspective, while mine is from neoclassical economics (history of economic thought).

1 Problems of Chinese Economy

1.1 Silver Standard

From the 1870s on, leading countries like Germany, France, USA began to join the gold club: shifting from centuries-long silver/gold bimetallism to the gold standard. This international trend was harmful to silver economies such as India, Japan and China: the purchasing power of silver devalued sharply. Worse is silver production increased in that period and the gold standard countries poured out their silver, further aggravated silver slump.

Following Book I Chap. 11 "Of the Rent of Land," there is a long "Digression concerning the Variations in the Value of Silver during the Course of the Four last

Centuries" (I.xi.d-I.xi.i, Smith: 195–234). Before translating this digression, Yan Fu described how China was damaged by being on the silver standard.

"As a silver standard country, gold, copper and corn prices in China rose significantly over the past decade. Since the Sino-Japanese War [1894], prices galloped even more seriously about one-third [around 1900]. Western countries were departed from silver to the gold standard, only China, India and Japan remained on silver. By now India and Japan are also on the gold standard, China is the only silver country. That is why silver flowed into China and gold flowed out, the result is silver price slump. But businessmen in China claimed that in major cities silver is still not abundant, why? Because since the Sino-Japanese War there were many railroads and other constructions, absorbed great quantity of silver, that is why silver scattered in this wide country and not easy to find. Silver price is determined by the international market, if silver is not dear in other countries, there is no reason that it is high in China. As to the high price of rice, it was due to population growth and export to foreign countries. As a general rule when an economy develops, the corn price will also rise, never fall. I heard some old-aged people saying that silver purchasing power dropped to one-third during the past two centuries; it dropped again 50% during the past 50 years. Anyway, it is harmful that China remained on silver while other countries shifted to gold, but this damage must has a bottom line. It is unattainable for China to shift to gold [due to insufficient foreign reserves and deep-rooted silver system], this is a major subject that affected all people from the Court to ordinary businessmen. We need able men who have broad perspectives to propose mature project" (pp. 206–7).

He wrote two other similar notes; one is when he translated the following sentences: "But to make any sudden change in the price of gold and silver, so as to raise or lower at once, sensibly and remarkably, the money price of all other commodities, requires such a revolution in commerce as that occasioned by the discovery of America" (Smith: 437). His note reads: "… the price of all commodities fluctuated so radically, an effect that was comparable to the time of the discovery of America" (p. 428).

The other note is on pp. 504–5 when he translated the following sentences: "… and in the discovery and conquest of Mexico and Peru …, she [Spain] presented them with something not very unlike that profusion of the precious metals which they sought for" (Smith, 1976: 565). Yan Fu was so concerned with the silver problem for two reasons. One is the decline of silver purchasing power vis-à-vis foreign commodities; two is the war reparations with Western powers that were singed on silver, but as silver slumped, China was asked to compensate the differences or pay in gold.

Why China did not strive to be on gold? Mainly due to insufficient foreign reserves. This is due to ever-present trade deficits aggravated by silver slump, the invasion of foreign manufactured goods and over-burdened war reparations. Several money doctors from the USA and the Netherlands made serious proposals to suggest China to adopt the gold-exchange standard (GES) like India and some developing countries: use gold vis-à-vis foreign transactions but use silver at home.

These proposals were not successful mainly because silver price rose (and gold price dropped relatively) after 1918 when the first World War was over (the gold club did not work during the 1914–8 War). So during the 1910s–20s, China was in dilemma: before 1914, it was beyond her ability to join the gold club, it was also too costly not to join it; after 1918, China might be able to adopt the GES, but the benefits were unpredictable because the prices of metals were fluctuating. It was therefore heatedly debated whether China should remain on silver or join the gold club or adopting GES.

It is argued that if China remained on silver between 1902 and 35, price and foreign exchange rate would have been more stable than if GES or gold standard were adopted. When Yan Fu was writing these notes (around 1900–1), China was mostly suffered from the silver standard; if he wrote these notes in the 1930s, he might feel fortunate that China remained on silver for the following reasons.

Eichengreen (1992) suggests that the 1929 Great Depression was mainly caused by the international gold standard: "The gold standard of the 1920s set the stage for the Depression of the 1930s by heightening the fragility of the international financial system. The gold standard was the mechanism transmitting the destabilizing impulse from the United States to the rest of the world" (p. xi). That is why Keynes described the gold standard as "golden fetters."

If Eichengreen's argument is applicable, then China would have been suffered by the "golden fetters effect" if she adopted GES or joined the gold club. In retrospect, it was fortunate that China remained on silver to be escaped from the 1929 Great Depression.

1.2 Lack of Standard in Measures and Specifications

Except for written form, few things have unified measures and specification in China: there are too many dialects, units of length, weight, etc., it remained so even today in non-official occasions.

> "But, first we cannot always judge of the value of the current money of different countries by the standard of their respective mints. In some it is more, in others it is less worn, clipt, and otherwise degenerated from that standard. ... Thirdly, and lastly, in some places, as Amsterdam, Hamburgh, Venice, &c. foreign bills of exchange are paid in what they call bank money; while in others, as at London, Lisbon, Antwerp, Leghorn, &c. they are paid in the common currency of the country" (Smith, 1976: 477–9).

To this Yan Fu commented: "This kind of thing is rare in Europe, but it happened so frequently in China. ... It has been a very long history that China lacked a unified measure of length etc. It has been said that the length of a "foot" in China just like the length of ten fingers [of various size]. This kind of unnecessary trouble cost little when seen individually, but as a nation the total costs are considerable, and this certainly hindered economic development. It also caused questions of moral hazard [cheating]. In a civilization of four thousand years like China, if this most urgent economic problem cannot be resolved, then there is no hope for other problems" (p. 477).

1.3 Trade Deficits

> "Nothing, however, can be more absurd than this whole doctrine of the balance of trade, upon which, not only these restraints, but almost all the other regulations of commerce are founded. When two places trade with one another, this doctrine supposes that, if the balance be even, neither of them either losses or gains; but if it leans in any degree to one side, that one of them loses, and the other gains in preposition to its declension from the exact equilibrium. Both suppositions are false. A trade which is forced by means of bounties and monopolies, may be, and commonly is disadvantageous to the country in whose favour it is meant to be established, as I shall endeavour to shew hereafter. But that trade which, without force or constraint, is naturally and regularly carried on between any two places, is always advantageous, though not always equally so, to both" (Smith, 1976: 488–9).

Yan Fu's comments are remarkable: "There were many arguments on economic policies both in Asia and Europe, it is usually not easy to determine which side is correct. However, the view in favor of protectionism and trade balance is nothing correct but totally wrong. The mercantilists pursuit trade balance in the view that trade is something like war: one's gain is another's loss. The Europeans hold this view since thousands of years, they were awaken after Smith's ideas prevailed. This shows how difficult it is to awaken the people. Since the opening of Chinese ports to foreigners, trade was dominated by Western powers; however, trading with foreigners was not the decision of our government, but was forced by foreign powers. The view of trade deficits prevailed in China since about half a century ago and still influential today as held by some leading political figures. This trade balance view was hold by British economic policy makers before Smith, and still hold by major figures of Smith's time, so it is unnecessary to blame people having the same view in China. Smith's doctrine on trade balance was very beneficial to Europeans, although his view is somewhat old in Europe, it is still new and striking to our country, and that is why I emphasize this passage to readers" (pp. 478–9).

The problem in Smith's time was that, with her trade superiority, England overaccumulated silver/gold from trade partners. This means excessive monetary supply in England, and the consequence was domestic price will be too high to weaken her foreign competitivity. To a country like China who suffered seriously from trade deficits and silver slump, Smith's anti-trade balance view is not suitable for China.

1.4 Tax Corruption

> "Some part of the public revenue of China, however, is said to be paid in this manner [in kind]. The mandarins and other tax-gatherers will, no doubt, find their advantage in continuing the practice of a payment which is so much more liable to abuse than any payment in money" (Smith, 1976: 839).

Yan Fu agreed: "In Smith's time Europeans already know this kind of thing about China, they certainly know much more today. The basic feature of taxation in China is 'to maximize tax levy from the local sources, but minimize submission to government

1 Problems of Chinese Economy 59

treasury'." He made similar observations about tax farmers in China (page 924), showing the inefficiency of taxation, and the abusing power of tax farmers.

1.5 Public Debt

In Book V Chap. 3 "Of publick Debts" Smith discussed how the government may help the state finance and improve the commerce and industry by utilizing well-designed public debts. The problem of public debts in China was so serious that Yan Fu had the following comments: "Readers having seen Smith's ideas in this chapter may reflect the situation of this issue in China. Should we do this way or that way? It is clear that we do not need any advice to decide what we should do. Our country is seriously suffered since recent years, the industrialists and businessmen were also in bitter situations, the nation also burdened by debts. ... What was worse is the Boxer Rebellion [1900] such that China owes tremendous reparations to foreign powers, and this aggravated state finance deficits. ... It is often said that a reform is unavoidable: if it is not done by Chinese, it will be done by foreigners. I heard this before and now see it happening" (p. 937).

A few pages later (pp. 943–5), he wrote a two-pages note to emphasize the seriousness of public debt in China.

(1) The conservatives think that was the result from trade with foreigners, so they propose to close all ports. Yan Fu refute these ideas: "...the old-fashion thought blamed foreign trade as a source of deficits, thinking foreign powers as blood-sucking vampires, ... if they read Smith's ideas and his great insights and still keep their old views, then they are hopeless." I am not in this opinion. The causes and the nature of public debt in China were so complicated and so threatened by foreign invasions, they were very different from the situations of England in Smith's time; even after reading Smith's book, I still do not think that will help China's debt problems.

(2) Reparations were the main causes of debts. "Previous reparations [e.g. the Opium Wars in China during the 1840s–50s] were still within the ability of Chinese state finance, no foreign debt was necessary. However, from the Sino-Japanese War [1894] we lost Korea and Taiwan and paid tremendous reparations, the revenues of custom were used for that purpose. ... Unfortunately, the Boxer Rebellion in May of this year [1900] was a disaster than anything happened before, ... reparations to foreign powers are beyond the capacity of state finance."

(3) The per capita debt in England and France were higher than China, but not "becoming poor due to debts," nor "therefore the nation declined" and "the per capita debt in China is less than one pound sterling, so we need no to worry about it." He rejected this reasoning later by pointing out that public debts in Europe and China are of different nature; the methods to repay debts are also different: "Debts in England and France were mostly spent for military expenses, their

army defended colonies and protected commercial interests. In this case, even if the debt was heavy, it is still profitable to raise more debts to earn more profits. By contrast, we were repeatedly defeated over the past decades, debts were mainly borrowed from foreign countries; these heavy debts created no benefits to people and helped nothing to state revenue. ... Although the sum of debt is similar in China and in European countries, the causes and the nature of debts are totally different: Debts in Europe are profit-creating, while debts in China were harmful, so how can we compare them on the same ground? ... Unless we have some radical changes from now on, not letting foreigners to manipulate our debts, I simply do not know the destiny of our nation."

These are heavy words, he grasped the essence of public debt problems. He made similar opinions of the same issue on page 959.

2 Economic Liberalism

Laissez-faire, anti-protection, free trade, anti-mercantilism, anti-regulation are the central message of Smithian liberalism. How Yan Fu commented and responded?

2.1 Anti-protectionism

In his translator's Foreword Yan Fu responded: "Policies on protection and monopoly are not rules for the general public nor fitting the spirit of justice, they also hindered the development of domestic commerce, and that is why economists were so against. It should be, however, careful to reform: no matter how wrong the old rules were, and how beneficial the new rules are, unavoidably some people will feel uncomfortable and suffered. That is why reform is always difficult and often bloody."

Some 140 pages later, he spent a full page to explain the effects of anti-protectionism: "Following the spread of Smith's book, the perception of Europeans on protectionism had altered greatly. Thereafter, the public opinions in England during a century were diagnostically changed, they began to oppose what Smith had attacked: businessmen finally fully understood that protective policies were harmful and caused disadvantages. They were in favor of abolishing tariff protection, in favor of equal opportunity for domestic and foreign commodities; exempting heavy duty for imported goods. Cartels and coalitions were eliminated gradually, and now almost not existing. ..." (p. 147).

However, there were still forces resisting these reforms; he explained that landlords were organized to push the government for more rights; to balance the situation, the government allied with other parties to act against the landlords, etc. "Where there are interests, people resist reform" (p. 148).

2 Economic Liberalism
61

Nearly 450 pages later (Book IV Chap. 7 "Of Colonies"), he took the topic again: "When Smith wrote these passages (around 1774–5), North America was about to be independent, that's why Smith was so serious about it: policies on protection and monopoly must be abolished, but the reform would be costly. In retrospect, Smith over-worried about the situation, what he said did not happen. Unexpectedly, for the state revenue of England, most policies conducted by anti-mercantilists were resulted with great interests and little damage. The reason is quite straightforward: for businessmen and industrialists, when one more constraint was removed, the market added one more courage; in some particular cases inconvenience happened but only had limited effect. The removal of protective policies inspired the morals of citizen and induced new business … previous inconveniences were quickly disappeared. …" (pp. 596–7). He over-praised the positive effects and underestimated the resistant forces. As the later history showed, this one-side view is rather naïve.

2.2 Anti-monopoly

> The exclusive privileges of corporations, statutes of apprenticeship, and all those laws which restrain, in particular employments, the competition to a small number than might otherwise go into them, have the same tendency, though in a less degree. They are a sort of enlarged monopolies, and may frequently, for ages together and in whole classes of employments, keep up the market price of particular commodities above the nature price, and maintain both the wages of the labour and the profits of the stock employed about them somewhat above their natural price. (Smith, 1976:79)

Yan Fu wrote a one-page note (pp. 62–3) to explain what Smith meant and offered some arguments.

(1) On the advantages of free supply and demand and the disadvantages of monopoly. "The principle of the interaction between supply and demand has been known since ancient time, but it was Smith who developed this principle to such a refined level because he had considered things in a long-run framework. … Physics in Smith's time was not yet well developed, Smith learned from hydraulics that, like water, price will be converged to the natural level; and the method to reach this goal is to let it be [laissez-faire, laissez-passer]. Monopoly is something like to build a dam to keep water higher than its natural level, although the water is still but it is far away from the true level. … Smith thought that the monopolists will set the price at the highest level, and competition will make price at the lowest level. This is a 'natural' view, its basic principle will not be easily altered" (p. 62).

(2) Some monopolies may be beneficial to the society but in most cases they are more harm than good. "For instance, the monopolistic spice business in the Netherlands kept price higher than natural price; the salt monopoly in China made price several times higher. However, there are some counter-examples: the mail post system in Europe was very cheap even under monopoly, post

revenue also contributed to state income, and this would not be possible if run by private firms. In some industries that required heavy sunk costs, free competition does not guarantee cheaper price: people in England hate monopoly, they allowed several railway companies to compete, but the price did not therefore lowered. ... Modern economists distinguish two kinds of competition, one is external competition (competing for a new market area), and the other is internal competition (competing within a given market area): it is claimed that monopoly is allowed for external competition, but not allowed for internal competition. The above are various ideas for readers' information, they are not conclusive" (pp. 62–3).

This passage reflects Yan Fu fully understood that not every monopoly is harmful; and in terms of social welfare, competition is not always better than monopoly. He used Chinese tea exports to illustrate the benefits of monopolistic cartel. "The drawback of cartel coalition is they controlled everything such that one cannot distinguish between good from bad. Suppose the cartel is established for the public benefit of a certain place, and forbids any cheating behavior, then this kind of cartel may be beneficial. The tea industry in the Fujian province [where Yan Fu was born] is open to everybody that over-competition forced some minor businessmen to sale bad quality tea in order to earn living, or cheating foreign merchants. All these hurt the whole industry fatally. Since the recent twenty years tea industry in India prospered, and the Fujian tea was in depression. If some major tea firms in Fujian could organize a cartel and making rules to reject low quality tea and having a reliable trade mark to endorse the quality, then Fujian tea could compete with Indian tea, the lost market can be recovered" (p. 150).

Despite this cartel proposal, his basic concept regarding monopoly was this: except for some public enterprises, basically he opposed monopoly in privates. "In general terms, monopoly and cartel are beneficial to the related business and industries, but harmful to public interest. If we consider the overall effects of monopoly, we may observe some wasting [i.e. social welfare losses due to monopoly]. If the country is already weak and unable to resist foreign pressure, then foreign cheap goods may be invaded and selling for high price. Suppose there is an identical commodity, taking salt as an example: the salt sold by monopolized channels with high price will be easily defeated by the smuggled private salt with lower price. It is therefore evident that monopoly is possible when the country [economy] is closed, and certainly cannot be survived when free trade prevails" (p. 142).

He explained that after the abolishment of monopolies in England, trade volume with other countries increased significantly. "When protectionism prevailed in European countries, they set up all kinds of barriers or levy heavy taxes to hinder foreign commodities; in the end they realized that this was mutually harmful. After the publication of Smith's book, English relaxed all trade barriers (named as free trade), domestic monopolies were abolished soon thereafter. The environment was totally reformed, open competition means equal opportunity for everybody. ... From then on, all goods are free to produce and free to circulate, output increased hundred times than before, the whole nation prospered and citizen enjoyed the fruits. People now realized that Smith's ideas are perfect decent and cannot be altered" (p. 142). Yan Fu emphasized the positive effects of laissez-faire, but did not tell readers why protectionism in England revived in the early nineteenth century (see Irwin's *Free Trade under Fire*, for a comprehensive study).

2.3 Economic Liberalism

> It is the highest impertinence and presumption, therefore, in kings and ministers, to pretend to watch over the economy of private people, and to restrain their expence either by sumptuary laws, or by prohibiting the importation of foreign luxuries. They are themselves always, and without any exception, the greatest spendthrifts in the society. Let them look well after their own expence, and they may safely trust private people with theirs. If their own extravagance does not ruin the state, that of their subjects never will. (Smith, 1976: 346)

To this beautiful argument, Yan Fu also added an elegant note: "… a major difference is that in modern time the State is the public servant to people, while in ancient time the sovereigns were parents of people. … Paternalism considers people need supervision and help, but by the name of assistance the State actually fettered people's activities; the beneficial measures provided by the State, paradoxically, disturbed people; the more policies provided by the government, the more damages will be. That is a general phenomenon can be found in every continent. Later politicians understood that, as to economic affairs, it is better to let people do as they wish, the less the disturbance from the State, the more benefits will be resulted. All that needs to do is to establish rules to be followed by, and by so doing the whole society will be in harmony and opulence. The old lessons by ancient scholars told us: the best policy is to be in accordance with the natural trend; the second best way is to induce the people by interests; the third way is to instruct people what and how to do; the fourth way is to ask people to fit into the planned framework; and the worst is to compete interests with the people" (pp. 346–7). This argument, his style and the old lessons he cited must have attracted readers of both new and old generations.

It is interesting to see how Yan Fu understood the meaning of free trade: "…The best interests of the sovereign is to let his subjects having stable income yearly, and increasing the availability of necessities. To attain this goal, a best way is to let the trade free. The advantage is obvious: allowing the maximization of the nation's output, merchants can be fairly competed, and commodity price will be most reasonable. … If all these were done, it is implausible that the nation is not prospered and the sovereign is not rich. By contrast, if the ruler has some particular ideas in mind and making unfair rules such as protection and monopoly, such that his subjects are easily offend the laws, then the consequence is high price level and everything will have the opposed effects as described above" (pp. 635–6).

In a note on page 469, he showed another understanding of liberalism. The operation of liberalism is not merely depend on the subjective willing of the ruler and/or his subjects; it requires many other conditions to make it happen: the favorable structure, the competitivity of commodities, the intellectuals background favored this laissez-faire spirit, etc. When these conditions were satisfied in England in the mid-eighteenth century, even if there had no such a man named Adam Smith who wrote WN, there certainly had another man writing a book of another name to advocate similar doctrines. Yan Fu fully understood that WN (and Smith) was a product of that epoch and economic liberalism predictable in that period.

Having this excellent understanding in mind, he tried to persuade readers about the suitability of Smithian liberalism to China. He did not develop a full length argument but only with the following brief sentences at the end of a note on page 469: "...People are worrying about the situation of China today and thinking it might be hopeless, ...I think the problem is that we underestimated our own intelligence, and have no full knowledge about ourselves. The drawbacks of monopoly etc. are in fact not a serious problem in China."

It is not persuasive in this insufficiently argued note. Moreover, I do not think Smith's liberalism fits Chinese economy: British laissez-faire, as said above, was a product of Empire with trade superiority; while Chinese economy around the 1900s was very weak, suffered from silver slump, trade deficits, foreign commodity invasion. A man's feast can be another's poison.

3 Other Comments

3.1 Anti-commerce and Pro-agriculture

We now understand the anti-mercantilism that Smith expressed in Book IV was to against social welfare losses due to monopoly and protectionism. But to Chinese readers who had no background knowledge in European economic history, it would be easily to reduce this anti-mercantilism message to anti-commerce and pro-agriculture policy that prevailed in Confucian mentality. This misunderstanding is strengthened when readers see the title of Book IV Chap. 9 "Of the agricultural System, or of those System of political Oeconomy, which represent the Produce of Land, as either the sole or the principal Source of the revenue and Wealth of every Country."

In the mid-eighteenth century, agriculture was a main source of national wealth both in England and in France; Smith naturally emphasized the importance of agriculture in this chapter. Book IV Chap. 9, taken from its face value, fits perfectly most Chinese readers' mentality: a country like China should emphasize on the agricultural sector and discourage the speculative commercial activities, even the great Smith said so.

For Yan Fu this was absolutely a misunderstanding, and totally opposed to what he had in mind. In the translator's Foreword, he explained: "In his book Smith sometimes expresses excessive criticism of merchants that readers in our time would feel to be exaggerated. But we should also be aware that merchants in Smith's time were not the kind we see now. Custom revenues were in the hands of certain corporations, who used national tariffs as a means of making profits; the high costs of the Seven

Years' War were partially financed by the East India Company, and business and politics were viciously inter-connected. Wars in America were expensive and were fought mainly for the interests of commercial groups; Congressional representatives were nominated by negotiation; tax rates were set in conspiracy between merchants and decision makers. This seriously damaged British laws and institutions at home. The various interest groups seldom care about the nation, as Smith so acutely shows in his book" (pp. 4–5).

When he was translating WN in 1900, the agricultural sector in China suffered from serious problems: overpopulation, diminishing return, scale diseconomy, etc. In short, it was in a state that now termed "agricultural involution": marginal productivity became negative but capital and labor inputs still continued. It is economically inefficient but farmers will be starved if they do not farm the land.

So Yan Fu was needed to argue: (1) WN was written in 1776, Smith's pro-agriculture idea is not applicable to today's England nor China. (2) The anti-commerce mentality was a mistake: in ancient time when China was strong and prosperous, policy was well balanced between the two sectors. (3) It was the misinterpretation of later mandarins and unorthodox Confucians who claimed that agriculture is the only source of wealth, and that commerce is unproductive and speculative (note in p. 57).

He repeated to advocate this pro-industry, pro-commerce orientation several times and blamed the present policy makers did not realized what China really needed (in the notes of pp. 91, 144, 364–5, 769). In these notes, he extensively quoted Confucian classics, his rhetoric skill and powerful arguments in his elegant style is attractive, but it is not easy to say if he had convinced them.

3.2 Saving or Prodigality?

> "Capitals are increased by parsimony, and diminished by prodigality and misconduct. ...Parsimony, and not industry, is the immediate cause of the increase of capital. Industry, indeed, provides the subject which parsimony accumulates. But whatever industry might acquire, if parsimony did not save and store up, the capital would never be the greater" (Smith, 1976: 337).

Yan Fu wrote three notes (between p. 336 and p. 341) to discuss the relationship between saving and consumption, three points stand out.

(1) The importance of saving. "In the traditional thought of the Taoist, parsimony is considered as a precious thing, indeed! But many people today dislike this idea and reject it, I do not understand their reasons. Smith told us that parsimony is the parents of the society, but by parsimony alone is not sufficient to support the society. The importance of parsimony is from which something will be raised or produced. If not for producing or raising something, then parsimony is nothing but money worms, cannot do anything useful to the wealth of nation and the opulence of the people" (p. 339).

(2) Some prodigality is unnecessary, but some are necessary. "Some said: prodigality hurts oneself but helps industries and commerce. This is a strange argument. The benefits of prodigality are limited to certain houses, if we take the whole society as a whole, these fortunes are wasted and never return, exhausting the limited resources. ... Today many nations spend millions and millions in military expansion, ... the expenses for justice and supervision are also high, ... it would be greatly beneficial if these expenses were saved and used for welfare, but these prodigality are necessary" (pp. 339–40).

(3) However, parsimony by poor citizen is meaningless. "Until recently Russia was a quite poor country, the parsimony by the poor small farmers is incomparable to the prodigality of the riches and nobles, so capital stock in Russia became exhausted and foreign debts increased. This is an exception to Smith's parsimony principle" (p. 341).

The problem in Russia was the socio-economic structure in which nobles and serfs were on unequal footings, this was very different the case of England. Living under unreasonable structure, "people's parsimony is ineffective to save themselves" (p. 337), because the accumulated capitals were used inefficiently (he had another similar note in p. 78).

3.3 War and Economy

> The manufacturers, during the war, will have a double demand upon them, and be called upon, first, to work up goods to be sent abroad, for paying the bills drawn upon foreign countries for the pay and provisions of the army; and, secondly, to work up such as are necessary for purchasing the common returns that had usually been consumed in the country. In the midst of the most destructive foreign war, therefore, the greater part of manufactures may frequently flourish greatly; and, on the contrary, they may decline on the return of the peace. They may flourish amidst the ruin of their country, and begin to decay upon the return of its prosperity. (Smith, 1976: 444–5)

This passage touched a pain point for Yan Fu: the manufacturers in England benefited from wars, while China was seriously ruined by wars. "Most Chinese wars were domestic and highly destructive. Many European wars were in foreign countries, such as in India, Turkey, Span and South Africa; European people did not suffer from these destructions. On the contrary, their industries and commerce were therefore expanded, many were thereby enriched. Another example is America's Civil War, the country was broken but the economy was prospered. A basic reason was military demand increased many times more than in peace time; the suppliers earned unusual profits. ... As the war ended, military demand declined sharply, tax rate increased in order to repay the public debts for the war, and that is why when the war ended the economy was depressed. This is the case of foreign war; in the case of domestic war, everything is destroyed" (p. 437).

3.4 Economic Mentality of the Mandarins

When translating Book V "Of the Revenue of the Sovereign of Commonwealth", he had several criticisms toward mandarins regarding their mentality and their way of making decisions. His key points:

Physiocracy. "Modern mandarins familiar with the view that the root of national wealth is in the agriculture. There are varied views on the reforms, some are favorable and some are against, but none is against the development of agriculture. In their view, there are still many unexplored lands in every province and many people remain unemployed, why not organize people to explore these lands? This is certainly a good suggestion but I think they only see one side of the problem: why the lands remain unexplored? And why poor people are not interested? If there are interests, no one will wait; it is simply because it is not profitable that these lands are idled" (p. 858). By this, Yan Fu means the mandarin should try to create opportunities in industries and commerce for the people, not confining to the agricultural sector.

Close-mindedness. "Mandarins know about agriculture, they also inclined to close-up the country to reject exchanges with foreigners. They also hate everything related to telegram, railway, foreign trade etc. ... To improve the State finance, a basic keyword is to do foreign trade, it is impossible that one wants to enrich the country but hate trade. ..." (pp. 858–9).

When the situation was chaotic, some policies were inappropriately taken. "The nation was (is) in disorder, some decision makers tried to issue new money in order to improve the difficult finance. The consequence was serious inflation under which poor people became poorer, and rich people were getting poor. ... I witnessed these changes and deeply regretful about the sufferings of our country" (p. 962).

Unfamiliar with foreign affairs. "Chinese intellectuals and mandarins were unfamiliar with trade and business, when foreign powers invaded and forced to open-up treaty ports, what mandarins can do was to sign the papers. They were unable to argue with foreigners, even if they tried, they did not know what to dispute" (p. 642). Another similar critique is that these mandarin "handle these foreign affairs with Chinese style, and was look down upon by foreigners. ...If they have any knowledge about the Western world, how could they negotiate with foreigners?" (p. 751).

4 Sources of Yan Fu's Ideas

Yan Fu's academic background was navy in the Fujian province before went to Greenwich (UK), where he stayed for two years. Even if he had some contacts of European social sciences while in England, within such a limited time it was not easy to know so much about sociology, politics, law, biology, logic, political economy as Table 1 in Chap. 1 shows. I suppose that his knowledge in social sciences was mainly self-taught, based on a general exposure while in England.

His knowledge in political economy, as reflected in his WN and 310 notes, I have the following observations. First, he knew major names in this disciples (such as Malthus, Jevons, Walker, Marshall); he also knew how economists used calculus as tool for analysis and using induction and deduction as methods of logical reasoning (see Appendix A).

Second, his knowledge in Chinese economic history and thought was also impressive: in many notes, he widely cited classics to explain that something similar also happened in China, or some important figures also have similar thoughts. This is an effective strategy to attract and convince.

Third, in many places he cited the editor's notes to the third edition of WN (1784) prepared by Thorold Rogers (1823–90). There are, however, in many places Yan Fu did not cite Rogers, but he was able to offer precise information. For instance, in the note on p. 212, he pointed out that the wheat price in WN was incorrect, and offered the correct price. I suppose his many background knowledge regarding European economic history were taken from Rogers' notes, either acknowledged or not.

Overall, even if one might disagree with his arguments or views, or find mistakes in his translations/notes, his knowledge in political economy around 1900 as we have seen in this chapter is quite remarkable.

Chapter 7
Epilogue

Reading Yan Fu's translation of WN (1902) more than a century later, what kind of reflections can one make? Two issues may be considered. (1) Intellectually speaking, how the intelligentsia reacted to the books that Yan Fu have translated in general (Table 1 in Chap. 1) and WN in particular? (2) In terms of policy, the ideas of minimum government, laissez-faire, free trade as advocated by Smith, were they suitable/useful in the 1900s?

1 Response

The famous scholar Hu Shi (1891–1962) was originally named Hu Honzi until he read Yan Fu's translation (1898) of *Evolution and Ethics and other Essays* by T.H. Huxley. He was so impressed by the notion "survival of the fittest" and decided to change his name to 'Shi' (fit). Hu recalled in his famous memoir *Self Portray at Forty* (*Sishi Zishu*): "I have two classmates, one named Sun 'Jingcun' (competition for survival), another named Yang 'Tianze' (natural selection). My own name was a souvenir of that particular epoch."

The famous self-made historian Qian Mu (1895–1990) told us in his *Teachers and Friends* (*Shiyou Zhayi*, 1983: 69–70) how he studied Yan Fu's translations seriously: "… [my senior friend] Chungli took a book from his shelf and said 'I was long intended to read this book but could not find time. Could you try to read it?' It was Yan Fu's translation (1903) of H. Spencer (1873): *Study of Sociology*. I said 'Very fine'. … I returned to school and read, looking up in the dictionary as Chunli instructed, and pasted some hand-written notes in the book. There were too many vocabularies that I was not familiar, it was shameful to write too many notes to show Chungli, so I stopped looking up in the dictionary and speeded up the reading perfunctorily. I went to Chungli's with that book, he asked me about its main ideas and my comments. He listened to me while standing up and showed some delights from time to time. …From then on he was much closer to me with some respect, praised me that I was a good reader with insights that many people usually did not perceive. ... He said, 'Fine, take one book with you as usual." I said, "I would like to continue reading Yan Fu's series, so I took his translation (1903) of *On Liberty* by John Stuart Mill. ... After these two books, I read all other books translated by Yan Fu, nevertheless I was most impressed by the first two; and I have to thank Chungli for this opportunity."

Not everybody appreciated Yan Fu and his translations; a well-know critique was made by Zhang Taiyan (or known as Zhang Bingling, 1868–1936), a famous scholar-revolutionary, in an article titled "Comments on *A Short History of Politics*" (by E. Jenks, 1900; Yan Fu's translation 1904), published in a revolutionary magazine *Minbao* in February 1906, No. 12.

Some literal excerpts. "*A Short History of Politics* by a British citizen Jenks, translated by Yan Fu, ... every scholar knows that Jenks's book has no great value, and Yan Fu praised Jenks's doctrines with some corresponding features of the Chinese society. ... There are many vulgar people in our society respect Yan Fu, and many politicians used Yan Fu's sayings to fool the whole nation. It was mainly because most people did not know who is the true Yan Fu. He studied in Western country during his youth, he was impressed by their race [European] and looked down up our yellow race, ... The uninformed people were impressed by his knowledge of European languages and his skillful expressions in classical Chinese style, and this kind of impression encouraged the spread of his dangerous ideas. ... In fact, although he is familiar with some Chinese classic works, but for a major part of Chinese learning he has only some superficial understanding. ... His knowledge of Chinese history is particularly weak, no more than some common senses. He only memorize some fragmentary facts while unaware of the whole background of its situation. In reading his translations of Western works, we see he was always delighted to remark those tiny things that are similar between China and the West. If it is a particular event or phenomenon in China, or there is any conflicting things between China and the West, then Yan Fu says nothing. Historical facts that fit his model are all true, otherwise all false. ... Testing Jenks's theory by evidence from China, we see the defects of his doctrines, Yan Fu nevertheless praised Jenks's ideas with his own judgments; what is worse is some politicians over-interpreted Yan Fu's folly words...."

There are many more harsh sentences that Zhang attacked Yan Fu in that article. People familiar with Zhang's personality are not surprised. This example shows that not every Yan Fu's contemporary loved him. Contrary to Zhang, I would like to defend Yan Fu from a "sympathetic understanding" point of view.

(1) His knowledge in Western humanities and social sciences was self-taught. Even if he had some defects as Zhang criticized, who else in China around the 1900s could translate these Western books of various disciplines? and with an elegant classic style that attracted such a wide readership?

(2) Could Zhang translate a valuable book with notes as Yan Fu did? With space constraint, Yan Fu could only simplify his ideas and comments within a few lines. His 310 notes are informative for our analysis.

(3) Yan Fu's main purpose was translations, not making his own arguments or writing short essays; although sometimes he was doing "more interpretation than

translation." As shown in Category 3 of Table 1 in Chap. 4 and the analysis in Sect. 3 Chap. 5, he was certainly not an uncritical translator.

(4) His translations, notes and his ideas are discussible/debatable, but he was certainly not a simple-minded follower of Western authors as Zhang criticized. It must have been a great fortune for China if there had another hundred scholars like Yan Fu in the 1990s.

Let us now turn to the receptions of WN in particular. To my best knowledge, materials in this regard are quite limited; the most famous comment was made by the famous Liang Qichao (1873–1929) in the very first issue of a magazine *Sinmin Zongbao* (*New Citizen Journal*, published fortnightly 1902–7). It is a four-paragraph book review (about 1500 words); in the lengthy first paragraph, Liang explains the significance of WN in Western economics and its main contents.

"Yan only translated the first two Books, the rest three Books are yet to be published." What Liang read was a preliminary version of the Book I and II appeared in 1901, but he was bold enough to judge that "the essential part of that work [WN] is in the first two books" before he read the complete translation (Liang was unable to read English). Liang states that "If readers could master them [Books I and II], then the foundation of this discipline is established; this will be helpful to read other economics books."

This is overstated because even if one masters WN (and WN only), it is not easy to follow Alfred Marshall's *Principles of Economics* (1890): there are new analytical apparatus such as geometry, algebra; as well as new conceptual devices such as marginal (utility, productivity) analysis that an only WN reader cannot follow.

In the second paragraph, Liang presented Yan Fu's style as: "In addition to textual translation, Yan Fu added many notes; most of them are new doctrines to compensate the deficiencies of Smith's text. This enlightened readers and demanded their ability to judge among competing doctrines, hence indeed a beneficial read. A problem is he translated many foreign terms with words chosen from classic Chinese, it is not easy to follow if one reads them with modern eyes. However, I think these terms translated by Yan Fu will be followed in other translations in this field [political economy]."

The third paragraph is an overall evaluation. "Mr. Yan is a first rank scholar both in Chinese and Western studies, he devoted several years to work out this translation and with many revisions, its superior quality is not the question. What I regret is its style: it is too concise and elegant, a style of ancient pre-Han classic, such that readers with insufficient classic training would be difficult to follow. WN is not an easy book to understand, it would not be beneficial to students if not presented in fluent style. Translation is aimed to diffuse ideas for citizens, not aimed to produce an immortal work to be read by limited elite. This is a bad habit among Chinese intellectuals, and I shall not hide this point even toward the respectable Yan Fu. I have two suggestions: one is to prepare a list of Glossary to contrast English and Chinese terms, this will facilitate readers to check the English version of WN as well as for later translators to follow Yan Fu's terms to avoid confusing terminology for the same word. Second, to prepare an introductory chapter to describe a brief history of this discipline [political economy], to show various schools of thought before and after Smith, and the historical significance of WN in this context. A general survey will benefits readers greatly. The present translation contains no preface, nor any information about who Smith was and when WN was originally published; this is an obvious shortcoming."

The fourth paragraph is irrelevant to WN. Yan Fu's reply appeared in No. 7 of that same magazine in 1902. In the first two paragraphs, he explains the difficulties of translating Western works into Chinese; in the final third paragraph, he answered two concrete questions.

(1) It is really not easy to prepare a glossary at this stage, for this is a huge book and there are too many entries that one needs a monograph to meet this requirement. This was done much later in the new edition by The Commercial Press in 1931; it contains 80 pages in the end of volume III, in which new editors had hard times to decipher, and in many occasions, names and terms are still not identified.

(2) Yan Fu explains that he had prepared a short biography on Smith and an introduction to explain his motivation and the contents of WN. That his drafts have been well revised and a complete version will be appeared in April or May (1902). Limited evidence is available to show the receptions of WN in China, but from many indirect sources, we know many intellectuals knew the laissez-faire ideas Smith advocated.

Yan Fu's translation of Huxley's *Evolution and Ethics* was so striking to Chinese that his translation of *The Wealth of Nations* (note that how this title may attract eyes) is unsurprisingly will be noted. There were some difficulties, however.

(1) Political economy was a new discipline for China, people could easily associate it with a book of money-making, and that is not to be welcomed by conservative readers. (2) Most readers had no sufficient background to understand WN, especially with Yan Fu's over-elegant style. (3) Plus Yan's unusual perceptions of WN as analyzed in Chaps. 4–6. (4) A major source of spreading Smith's ideas came from, again, Lain Qichao's summary of WN in his *A Concise of History of Economic Thought*[1] (see Appendix C).

The impact of WN in China during Yan Fu's lifetime was reasonably limited. When western economics was introduced from Europe and Japan decades later, new doctrines (both neoclassical and Marxian) easily superseded this 1776 book.

2 Evaluation

Three related issues: (1) Were Smith's ideas an appropriate prescription to cure China's unfavorable situation? (2) Why the intellectual and political milieu reacted passively to Smith's ideas? (3) What were the opinions held by other intellectuals concerning Chinese political economy?

---

[1] Liang wrote chapters of this book and published in various issues of his *Sinmin Zongbao* in 1902. Wang and Trescott (1988) translated this brief book: 61 pages in total in which 22 pages were on Western economic thought prior to Smith, and 14 pages on Smith's work and its implications.

After the Opium War of 1840, the economy was invaded by Western industrial products and the international payments were in serious deficit due also to reparations and foreign debts. The situation was somewhat similar to that of Germany and Japan in the early nineteenth century: basically an agricultural economy and conservatism prevailed in the ruling class.

Under such a similar situation, what China should have learned is from these two living examples by adopting a (tariff) protection policy in order to develop light industry (known as "import substitution" in modern development economics). The policy advocated by the German National Economy School (such as Friedrich List, 1789–1846) should be a good doctrine for China.

The anti-mercantilism and liberalism doctrines in France and UK had their particular background during the fifteenth–seventeenth centuries; men in industries and commerce, intellectuals were in favor of that orientation, and it was this tendency that made WN famous: its publication was a mature time to give a *coup de grace* to the until now dominant mercantilism. What Yan Fu introduced was a policy of laissez-faire and free trade, which were the products of that particular epoch.

But for China who had very different structure and historical roots, it is logically inappropriate to introduce such a doctrine from a "core" economy (England) to a periphery (China), without critique or adjustment.

List was not against free trade blindly. In his view, it is necessary to establish a "national economy" (protectionism against foreign powers) before talking about "world economy" (free trade among nations). His development plan for Germany was: (1) encourage within-state free trade, to develop German economy with a particular emphasize on the agriculture sector. (2) With protectionism measures to develop infant industries, fishery industry and foreign trade. (3) Until certain degree of maturity in national economy, free trade policy with the rest of the world will be taken. In his view, UK was at stage (3) while Germany and the USA were still at stage (2), hence inappropriate to follow Smith's guidance.

It is quite possible that Yan Fu was not aware of this German school. England at that time was the mainstream of intellectual activity; it is possible that Yan Fu simply translated a famous book from an admirable Empire, without prior knowledge about the historical and operational meanings of WN, and its inappropriateness for China.

As to the second issue, it seems that the intellectuals and political milieu did not react warmly to WN. Socially speaking, for new intellectuals, as Liang also felt, Yan Fu's text was hard to follow, and the contents of WN were just too remote. For traditional and conservative, they simply disliked and rejected books concerning "interests and profits" (money-making), such as the title *Wealth of Nations* indicated.

Politically speaking, some of the mandarins in the Court were more realistic than Yan Fu. They had taken some important measures such as establishing steel factories, shipping companies, industrial manufactories in order to compete with foreign firms and imported products. The ideas of free competition, laissez-faire from WN were not practical or even strange for them.

The third issue is: What were the opinions held by intellectuals regarding economic policy? It would be sufficient to cite, again, Liang who wrote in the end of his Chap. 5 of his *A Concise of History of Economic Thought* (1902):

Although mercantilism hindered economic development in Europe in the 16th century, it seems to be the only remedy for today's China. With rich natural resources, China can be self-sufficient in her daily needs. Therefore, a tariff barrier against goods to be imported and a high price level of the imported goods will not affect the general living standard of the people. Having the cheapest labor force and a sufficient supply of raw materials, China is able to produce low cost commodities. It is therefore a good policy to encourage exports. Based on the experience of western countries, colonization contributes to domestic growth. So far China has no colony, it is advisable for the Chinese government to carry out a colonization and overseas adventure policy. Compared with European business in the 14th and 15th centuries, whose ability of doing business took a lot of government effort to foster, Chinese businessmen are more talented and enterprising. China is therefore expected to be more effective in implementing mercantilist policy. Unfortunately, no mercantilist statesman like Cromwell has ever appeared for hundreds of years in China. (translated by Wang and Trescott, 1988: 44–5)

Liang was eager to apply European mercantilism; his ideas were directly opposed to Smith's (and Yan Fu's) liberalism. There were people in favor of Smithian ideas, but I think the majority will agree with Liang's principles (active government and protectionism), although not all agreed his proposals, especially his idea about colony.

Taken together, the prescription Yan Fu introduced from Smith was not well received by intellectuals and policy-makers. Economic structure differences in China and UK pre-determined this conclusion. From the point of view of idea diffusion, most readers of WN did not thereby obtained a systematic knowledge of political economy through Yan Fu.

3 Final Remarks

Two major approaches to study history of economic thought. (1) The relativist regards every single theory put forward in the past as a more or less faithful reflection of contemporary condition, each theory being in principle equally justified in its own text. (2) The absolutist has eyes only the strictly intellectual development of the subject, regarded as a steady progression from error to truth. Relativists cannot rank the theories of different periods in terms of better or worse; absolutists cannot help but do so (Blaug, 1997: 2).

My study of Smith and Yan Fu is clearly a relativist approach: trying to understand how an intellectual product accumulated under a totally different culture system was absorbed into another culture system which had a different intellectual background (insufficient vocabulary and without corresponding concepts), but also had a huge gap in economic structure.

Something interesting happened in the translation and reception of WN in the 1900s China. One thing could be unusual in the case of Yan Fu: he added 310 notes (Table 1 in Chap. 4), from which we see his understanding, criticisms and praises toward WN (Chap. 5), these notes also revealed his own ideas (Chap. 6).

I have no intention to criticize Yan Fu's translations; on the contrary, he deserves full respect. "There are several books that if I am not engaged to translate, there will

3 Final Remarks

be no one can do within 30 years; even if they do with efforts, I am not sure if they can get the essentials. ...". This was not exaggerated when he wrote this undated letter (supposed to be before 5 April 1899) to his publisher of WN (reprinted in Yan Fu's collected writings, III: 525–6).

Yan Fu's distortions and over-interpretations are reasonable results under "unequal exchange" in cultural confrontations. Some readers may object to my criticism that Yan Fu should not have advocated Smithian liberalism as an effective means to save Chinese economy, but this is debatable.

Appendices

Appendix A: Foreword to the First Chinese Edition of *The Wealth of Nations* (1901)

What is now called economics in the West corresponds to what we call *Jixue* ("learning of state finance management") in Chinese. Etymologically "economy" comes from the Greek "oikonomia" with the meanings of management and calculation, derived from "the management of the households." It stems from the meaning of thrift in consumption and calculation in the process of production. Its meaning has since expanded into the planning and management of national production and expenditure.

Translated into Japanese, the term economics is *Jingji* (managing the nation and supplying the people). This broad term is used to indicate the wide range of this discipline. In Chinese, we translate it as *Licai* (management of finance). Precisely speaking, *Jingji* is too broad, and *Licai* is too narrow, so I use the term *Jixue* to denote economics. What I mean by *Jixue* is not limited to the narrow sense of "calculation"; it refers also to the broad sense of calculation in land production, supply and demand of food, natural resources, national accounting, etc.; it also refers to plan national budget, which corresponds well to the original meaning of "economy" in Greek. That is why I consider WN to be a book on economics.

Then, why do I use not *Jixue* but *Origins of Wealth* (*Yuan Fu*) as the Chinese title for WN? Well, the title used by Smith in fact emphasizes the nature and causes of national wealth; it thus seems appropriate that I use *Origins of Wealth* for the Chinese edition. Moreover, the contents and style of WN also differ from what is now called economics in two ways: first, WN is more a practice-oriented book than an economic theory oriented book; second, Smith put more emphasis on the correction of the "economic errors" of his time than on the discipline of economics itself. For instance, Chap. 2 and 3 of Book III and Chap. 5 of Book V are digressions on practical questions only indirectly related to economics, and we cannot consider these parts as a scientific discourse. As the title of WN indicates, the book was intended as an inquiry into the nature of profits and finance, the causes of wealth and poverty, and the sources of national revenue. That is why I maintain that WN is a book of *Jixue* rather than a book on scientific (orthodox) economics.

It is flattery to consider Smith as the founding father of economics. Discussions on finance and tax are widespread in many books in China and the West and do not originate in Western political economy. In Chinese economic history, one can easily find famous administrators in different dynasties who wrote treatises about market supply and demand, about eminent entrepreneurs, on particular economic events, on the monopoly of iron and salt, and so forth. Although there was no such systematic development of economic discourse as in the West, one cannot deny that there are some insightful observations in the history of Chinese economic activities. In the West, there were economic experts in ancient Greece and Rome. Smith's doctrines were influenced by his teachers and friends, such as Cantillon, Turgot, Hume, Hutchison, Locke, Montesquieu, Petty, and others, whose arguments about political economy we can see in this book (WN). The main emphasis of this book is on the doctrines of the physiocrats, which are indebted to the French intellectuals. What is particular in Smith is that he was able to pick up the essences of different authors and spell them out in a precise way, side by side with concrete examples. He used a practical style of analysis, and his rhetoric was so skillful that readers of various levels of intelligence can understand it. It is due to this book that people came to acknowledge that political economy can be regarded as an independent discipline. That is why Smith is regarded as the prime economist and the father of this new teaching.

In terms of science, economics is a science of induction. Induction means that one observes the changes, understands the rules of change, then spells out economic laws. Works by people such as Smith, Ricardo, Mill (father and son) all belong to this category. Recent works by scholars such as Jevons and Marshall gradually shifted to the method of deduction, using tools such as calculus and geometric presentation to infer the logic of economic phenomena. The reasoning of the discipline therefore became much more precise. This was a significant progress in political economy during the past two centuries. If readers want to understand economics in a more comprehensive sense, the works by Mill, Walker and Marshall must also be translated. Only after mastering these works is one safe from ignorance. Although I understand the importance of this task, it is beyond my ability. Our younger generation must have someone fulfill this need.

Since modern economics is much more precise and more deeply analytical, why do I choose an old book by Smith (1776)? First, because we need to know what happened before, and reading history is helpful for understanding our contemporary situation. Second, what blame Smith attributed to the administrators of his time in this book (WN) corresponds quite well to the mistakes committed by our economic decision-makers. WN is, therefore, a "mirror book" to reflect our errors. Third, as this book was written when Europe and Asia started to have contacts, it contains much information concerning British and French laws and institutions, which can be useful to us. Fourth, Smith's style is easily accessible, for he offers evidence for every principle which he advocates; some other political economy books, while clear in style and full of theoretical reasoning, are elegant but not easy for beginners.

Obvious "truths" are not always easy to understand if the timing is not right; sages and wise men are not always aware of simple realities. For example, nowadays, we consider gold (and precious metals) as the wealth of a nation; this was also so in Europe two centuries ago. From Adam Smith on, people became aware that gold is nothing but a commodity. It is a means (source) of investment, a source which all the people can use and share, the monopoly of none. From today's point of view, this is common sense and not hard to understand. However, had we been born at Smith's time, it is not certain that we would have held such a view; we might have been in agreement with the ideas of the time. A living example in China is commercial policy: free domestic trade policy (liberalizing commercial activities) was strongly debated among decision-makers twenty years ago, but now is a matter of national consensus. After a certain concept reaches consensus, it is easy to put it into practice. But before that day comes, there are long nights when incorrect concepts prevail; and during that time one needs unusual insights to unveil the truth. This process is not confined to economic affairs.

When people considered gold as the wealth of a nation, the strategy was to maximize the balance of trade, to export as much as possible and to minimize imports. The tactics used were replete with commercial barriers and even the protection of trade by military force. People did not realize that is not a key factor for the wealth or poverty of a nation. The whole of Asia is still obsessed with the idea of gold as wealth; it is a valuable thing that Smith unveiled this illusion two centuries ago.

Our current endeavor is to maximize trade surplus, protecting our merchant class, encouraging domestic trade and discouraging the competition of foreign commodities. England was an outstanding example of these kind of policy: exports were subsidized, there were rebates for export taxes, there were Navigation Acts to protect trade gains and so on. All of these were designed to increase British gold-wealth. However, why did England ultimately get no richer and lose its territories in America? It was due to Smith's book that people started to understand that under the name of "protection policy," the real effect was to create barriers to trade. Perhaps some traders benefited at certain times, but in the long run, such protective measures were hurting the wealth of the nation. Reactions and protests naturally arose; conflicts were widespread between rulers and merchants. Truth is not generated only by debates; it must also be evident from facts. Copernicus's doctrine is now fully accepted and no one can reject it; his theory is true when we project millions of years backwards, and it will still be true millions of years hence. We should not doubt the principles contained in Smith's book; we will benefit if we follow his principles and will be damaged if we do not.

Policies on protecting trade through the granting of monopolies in China are not impartial. Moreover, these policies can in fact damage the development of commercial activities. All people concerned with economic affairs are all critical of these policies. I think it is fair to criticize the policies, but since they are already in place, caution should be used when trying to replace them with alternative measures. For when people become irritated and emotional, policy-makers and the beneficiaries of these policies must be cautious about unpredictable incidents.

At the time of reform, decision-makers should proceed with particular caution, for people who have invested in business before could lose their assets, and long-established customs cannot be changed radically within a short time. So however bad the old laws are and however good the new deals, administrators must be careful not to enact the new laws in the morning and ask people to obey them in the afternoon. So much unnecessary damage is caused by such lack of coordination. That is why reform is difficult and has often been accompanied by bloodshed. That is a tragedy. Policy decisions are usually based on realities, but sometimes they caused unpredictable results. Thought and care must be given to proposing policies.

In his book, Smith sometimes expresses excessive criticism of merchants which readers in our time would consider exaggerated. But we should also be aware that merchants in Smith's time were not the kind we see now. Customs revenues were in the hands of certain corporations, which used national tariffs as a means of making profits; the high costs of the Seven Years' War [1756–73] were partially financed by the East India Company, and business and politics were evilly interconnected. Wars in America were expensive and were fought mainly for the interests of commercial groups; Congressional representatives were nominated by negotiation; tax rates were set in conspiracy between merchants and decision-makers. This seriously damaged British laws and institutions at home. The various interest groups seldom care about the nation, as Smith so acutely shows in his book.

Naturally, policy-making is based on facts, but the implication behind policies is never impartial. Once time has passed and the environment has changed, one feels that the writer was exaggerating. If a scholar uncritically accepts what he reads, it will do more harm than good. All practical arguments are valid only for a certain time and place; they can be good newspaper articles but should not be taken as scientific truth. What science needs are general rules or laws that are valid for any time and place.

What Smith attacked most in British economic affairs was the East India Company (EIC), which was the most important economic corporation of that time, both in terms of its business volume and in terms of British economic strategy. EIC was built-up by merchants during the time when the Mongolian dynasty in China was declining and the conflicts in India were heated. It is amazing that, within a few years, a particular group of (British) people occupied such an immense territory as large as China. They were more competent than Alexander the Great; even Anthony of Rome could point to no such achievement. Their success was so great that international observers watched their every activity. But in Smith's eyes, EIC was a strange combination: an economic organization which also played a significant role in politics. It did not rule the people nor improve their standard of living; rather, its policies were harmful to the people, and it made unreasonable profits through the monopoly granted to it by the King. This kind of behavior is no different from national theft, but EIC was under state protection. A sage's insights are not valid if they are only temporally; only when they are long-lived can we see his real wisdom.

Some critics claim that Smith's book defended the profit-making class. They worry that if an economist is preoccupied with profit calculation, then his theory and doctrines will be profit-oriented; and that if the profit-oriented theory prevails, then the whole of society will be endangered. This is a very severe criticism. One has to understand that the object of science is to present what is true and what is not true. One must examine whether the reasoning is logical or not, rather than judge it by one's subjective preference. Moreover, Smith was analyzing the methods of calculation and profit-making, not making profits for his own purpose. He exposed all kinds of possibilities so that people could learn from his book to prevent unnecessary pitfalls. The criticism is similar to reading a book on military tactics and holding the author responsible for invasions of other countries and the killing of people.

Smith proposed that the motivation for people to participate in a given group is not always goodwill. Any group must consist of four elements: food, wine, money and sex. Few people's activities are intended for the good of others—people are self-interested—but there is an accumulation process to assemble these self-interests into public welfare. Civilizations are made from self-interested behavior. This theory was abhorrent to moralists, which is why Smith regretted his self-interest theory and claimed that his ideas had changed; he also intended to burn some of his lecture notes.

There are many different editions of WN. This translation is based on the third edition (1784) annotated by Thorold Rogers, published by Oxford University Press (1869). Rogers himself was an economist, he provided some valuable data on British wheat prices and his annotations and corrections are especially useful. I have taken some relevant notes and translated them in this Chinese edition; I have also taken notes from other editions and commented on them with my own observations. I hope these can be used for further discussions among my readers.

My translation of this book is different from my translation of T.H. Huxley (1841): *Evolution and Ethics* (Chinese edition 1898). In translating WN, I abridged the original text after I fully understood Smith's arguments. I added nothing to the text but some passages are omitted. In Chapter 11 of Book I ("Of the Rent of Land"), there are some digressions on the fluctuation of silver prices during four centuries; this passage is full of details, and so I provide only some of its main points. From Chap. 3 of Book IV, some details on the banks in Amsterdam have been omitted. From Book I London's wheat prices between 1202 and 1829 (completed by Rogers) have been deleted. I have added a chronicle table to compare major events in China and in the West, hoping that it will help readers to understand the historical background.

Economics is an important discipline which influences China's wealth or poverty. From a different perspective, economics also matters to the destiny of the Asian peoples. That is why when I felt Smith's arguments were related to our current situation, or when his texts stimulated my sentiments, I have written down my comments as translator's notes. Sometimes, they contain strong arguments, but I could not stop myself from writing these long and pointed notes.

The mechanisms of "natural selection" and "survival of the fittest" work twenty-four hours a day. The resources in this universe are finite. Those who are intelligent share a major part of these resources; the disfavored and the weak have to survive with limited means. The affluence and poverty of a nation are determined by the same mechanism. One should not avoid talking about one's own defects; I do hope that Western science can be of help to the destiny of our unfortunate country.

Yan Fu

August 1901

Appendix B: Preface to the First Chinese Edition of *The Wealth of Nations* (1901)

Yan Fu has just translated an economics book by Adam Smith, with the Chinese title *Origins of Wealth*, and asked whether I can provide a preface. This book is widely known in Europe and America, but our country is still not aware of it. Yan Fu's translation is, therefore, indispensable.

Every country needs finances (money), and especially a country in crisis. The management of a country requires finances to facilitate administration. When a country is in danger, its financial situation is also in great deficit, and attempts to ensure the country's survival are often in vain. The question of finances is, therefore, particularly important when a country is in decline.

Traditional mandarins and intellectuals avoid talking about profits, money and interest. They are also steeped in the doctrine of "promote agriculture, oppress commerce"; the channels for creating more national wealth are thus often obstructed. Recently, the demand for finances has increased rapidly, but the wealth of our nation is scattered in various parts of the country without management or attention. If we disregard our own riches, then other countries will come to divide and share them as if they were entitled.

In fact, our country is now rejecting available national wealth, and not allocating resources to those who can use appropriately. What is worse is that administrators are still focused on the old and limited channels to finance themselves. These channels are quickly exhausted and the whole nation becomes embarrassed by financial deficits. The situation now is that our country is not in our own hands, and our wealth is in the hands of foreign powers.

Although the danger and the crisis are so obvious, people are not still seeking alternative strategies to alter this unfavorable situation; they merely stand and look at each other without doing anything positive. Some have tried to change things but failed to propose a feasible strategy; some have tried hard with different methods but finally without significant result.

Looking back in Chinese economic history, the good administrators of wealth and finance were in fact rulers who were thrifty. Bad rulers deprived the people of wealth for their own purposes; this is what we called "narrowing down the sources of wealth." Thrift is a good strategy for times of peace, when it can finance the administration and the wealth can be stored in warehouses. But this method is useless in times of crisis because there is nothing left to save. What is worse is that our production equipment is damaged, and also cannot be counted as assets. The vicious cycle repeats itself; the crisis grows deeper and deeper.

What can we do to change the situation? We can create wealth from our whole country with good management and not waste our resources in ignorance, this does not require particular talent; others have done it. What bars this possibility is people's mentality and customs. If rulers and administrators are still embarrassed to talk about profits and interest, and still fettered by the doctrine "promote agriculture, oppress commerce," they are unconsciously discarding the usable resources.

Under this constraint, how can we expect them to create wealth with good management? If one is ashamed of profits, then there is no way to develop knowledge of wealth management. If one is inclined to promote agriculture and oppress commerce, then the wealth to be managed will be meager. The function of commerce is to circulate the wealth; agriculture is but a means of creating wealth. Today people are closing the many channels of wealth creation and emphasizing only one source of wealth; they are indeed narrowing down the source. Unfortunately, our agricultural sector is now also in deficit.

In ancient China, there were many ways to create wealth. When wealth was abundant, commercial activities arose to circulate it. This is similar to taming a river (flood control): the water manager distributes water to different plants and fields, to adjust excesses and deficits, so that farmers need not try to meet their needs by themselves but can concentrate on production. Commerce has a similar function.

In ancient China, farmers could purchase fresh fish and meats, commodities circulated freely, and artisanal products were circulated. In this way, the wealth created from nature could be used and circulated, and thus commerce was encouraged. Every distribution route was open to merchants; there was no such absurd doctrine as "promote agriculture, oppress commerce."

This non-pro-agriculture policy created considerable national wealth, which was maintained until the time of Emperor Wu in the Han Dynasty (129-88BC). Commercial activities declined because the stock of gold (money) was exhausted. China used copper as a means of exchange for two thousand years, but the exploitable copper mines are now exhausted. Our current source of precious metals is insufficient. Our nation recently tried to reform, but a major problem is the financial deficits. Some people maintain that China is still the wealthiest nation in the world and that the problem of poverty is not our main worry.

Now it is an appropriate time for Yan Fu's translation of Adam Smith's book on profits and wealth to appear. Some current opinion is critical of merchants' commercial activities and refers to the Chinese "oppress commerce" tradition. I do not agree with this tendency, and that is why I have put forward such a pro-commerce argument. If you are inclined to Western economic policies, then you can find their main arguments in Smith's book; if you are inclined to traditional Chinese wisdom, please remember what I have said in this preface, which I hope will be helpful to the circulation of human power and national wealth.

Wu Rulun

November 1901

(two years before his death)

Comment

A major point in Wu's Preface is that the traditional Chinese anti-commerce mentality was a major obstacle to create national wealth, that this mentality had been absent in ancient China, and that it had appeared only since the Han Dynasty. He suggested that a balanced policy of agricultural and commercial growth was more appropriate. It is clear that he took in the free trade message of Smith's book, and he argued that this would be a good prescription for China's disadvantaged situation.

For today's reader, his point seems elementary and shallowly argued, but it should be noted that he had his "enemy readers" in mind. Both Wu and Yan Fu used a very elegant (but difficult) classical style to argue current economic problems and policy. It was a useful style to induce close-minded mandarins to read.

Appendix C: Liang Qichao's Comments on *The Wealth of Nations* (1902–4)

Structure

Liang wrote a long article "A Concise History of Economic Thought" which was initially published in *Xinmin congbao* (New Citizen Journal), a bi-weekly magazine that Liang created in Yokohama, Japan in 1902–7. It was appears in Nos. 7, 9, 13, 17, 19, 23 (may–December 1902) and No. 51 in August 1904; now collected in his *Essays*, volume 12, pp. 1–61. This long essay contains:

Foreword (pp. 1–2);

Introduction (pp. 2–5);

Chapter 1 "Historical development of economics" (pp. 7–11);

Chapter 2 "Economics in ancient time" (pp. 11–3);

Chapter 3 "Economics in the Middle Ages" (pp. 11–3);

Chapter 4 "Economics in the 16th century" (pp. 13–6);

Chapter 5 "The mercantile system" (pp. 16–22);

Chapter 6 "Economics in the 17th century" (pp. 22–4);

Chapter 7 "Economics in the first half of the 18th century" (there is only one line: "The period covered in this chapter is transitory, no truly innovative doctrine was developed although there were many different views; it would be clumsy to expose all these ideas as well as for the fear of readers might feel tiresome about all these, so I leave it in blank");

Chapter 8 "The Physiocrats" (pp. 24–8);

Chapter 9 "Adam Smith's doctrine" (pp. 28–43);

Appendix "The principle of balance of payments and its relevance to Chinese economy" (pp. 43-61).

The Appendix is the longest one (18 pages) but its contents have nothing to do with history of economic thought: Liang illustrated the components of balance of payment, how to calculate them, showed the corresponding statistics in China during the past 15 years and explained the factors that made the problem so serious. The nature of this Appendix and its length should be printed as an independent article.

The length of most chapters is within or about 5 pages. An important reason of the lengthy Chapter 9 (16 pages) is that Yan Fu's translation of *The Wealth of Nations* was just appeared (1902), but his style is so condensed that most readers faced two difficulties: the difficult Chinese text itself, and the highly condensed economic ideas that was totally new. As Liang put it: "There are less 1% of students accessed to this book, and less than 0.1% of readers who can understand it. It is truly lamentable. That is why I tried to provide some background information about Smith and summarize his doctrines for readers who intend to learn from this book (... I am acting as a guide to *The Wealth of Nations*)" (12:29).

From his initial plan presented in a Figure in pp. 6–7 (Wang and Trescott [hereafter as W&T] 1988:24), we see that several more chapters were scheduled but not completed:

(1) Smithian pessimism;
(2) Smithian optimism;
(3) Manchester school;
(4) J.S. Mill's and pre- and post-Mill theories;
(5) Non-Smithian school;
(6) New school: (a) historical school, (b) nationalism [?].

With today's knowledge of history of economic thought, the nine chapters up to Smith as illustrated above are basically sound and understandable. But it is difficult to find the corresponding categories in modern history of economic thought textbooks for the above (1), (2) and (3). Also, (5) is too broad to be understandable; and (6b) is also questionable.

It is quite possible that the table of contents in 12:6–7 was based on some books of this discipline published in Japan around 1900, either authored by Japanese scholars or translated from Western languages. A puzzle is why Liang did not mention

86   Appendices

Marxism and socialism? Japanese texts on both lines must have been abundant, perhaps Liang thought these are fashionable ideas, they are too early to be included in the history of economic thought.

Motivation

In his Foreword, Liang listed "seven points" to explain his motivation, the sources that he based, and explained the difficulties to do this kind of rendition mainly due to hard to find corresponding terminology in Chinese to convey the message appropriately.[1]

In his Preface to the Chinese version of WN (1902), Yan Fu's mentor Wu Rulun criticized that Chinese intellectuals and mandarins were shied away from things related to "interest" or "profit." The country paid high prices when the mandarins managed economic affairs clumsily: they were knowledgeable in classics but incapable to face foreign invasion. Wu tried to persuade readers that WN is not a book on interest and profit; it is highly related to economic policy.

Liang basically repeated this argument but in different form[2]: "The Confucians always saying that 'Why we need to talk about interest and profit? What we need is morality and justice'. ... They do not understand that justice and interest, righteous and utility are two sides of the same thing. ... We Chinese are famous in the world for the thirsty of profit, we are people of excellent in calculation and profit-seeking, the teaching of Confucian doctrines did not educated us to ameliorate this world view, ...most people often seek the present tiny interests at the expense of long-run considerable profits. It is not only a few men who committed this kind of error, almost everybody acts in this way, and that is why the power of China was declining. Western countries were developed only in recent centuries, although several reasons made them possible, the development of economic doctrines was one of the main reasons. ...we Chinese people do not know how to study economics, or even not know the very existence of it. It is something like someone situated in a dangerous situation but insensitive to it. ... readers should be careful enough not to consider Economics as a subject of seeking tiny profit" (22: 4–5).

Comments

Liang made five comments where he began the sentence with an "AN" which means remark, comment or footnote (12: 21–2, 33, 34, 35, 40). The final two ANs are brief

---

[1] The first four points are presented in Wang and Trescott pp. 19–20, Points 5–7 are not meaningful to Western readers because Liang discussed which term in Chinese is more appropriate for "Economics," and explained that he followed about 80-90% of Yan Fu's terminology used in the WN.

[2] The follow passage in not translated in Wang and Trescott p. 22, only sweepingly summarized in p. 23.

footnotes: (1) "AN: The view expressed by Smith on the fluctuations of interest rate has been corrected by Yan Fu in the lower part of Book I [I do not know which one] that I need not to quote" (p. 35).

(2) "AN: Recently Jenks [i.e. Jeremiah Jenks of Cornell University] proposed new currency system for China [i.e. the gold-exchange standard, 1904], his first principle is to limit the quantity of total money supply, the basic idea is based on Smith's view that summarized here."[3]

The first three ANs are long comments which contained two main arguments. The first one was to argue that the mercantile system that prevailed in Europe during the fifteenth–seventeenth centuries had its particular historical background and produced certain positive effects, but at the time of Smith (mid-eighteenth century), the disadvantages of this system were obviously much more than its benefits.

So Liang reminded readers that "while reading Smith's book it is necessary to consider the time and the overall background that he situated; what is important is to appreciate his ideas and motivations" (12: 34). His point was that "what Smith said were good for Europe of that time, but not for today's China" (12: 34).

"AN: The mercantile system in Europe after the sixteenth century was truly harmful to the development of European economy; but if this system were transplanted into today's China, it is truly the only way to save us" (12: 21). He developed this point in length (12: 21–2), but this argument is discussible.

The successfulness of mercantilism in England was not without costs: it required powerful navy to ensure the Navigation Acts, it required supports from the Parliament for the Corn Laws. How could China to have these conditions to compete with Western powers?

We now see better that Liang's understanding of mercantilism is rather superficial: "China has abundant population and lowest wage level, plus abundant with raw materials, ... Chinese merchants are also adventurous, ... so if we apply mercantilism to today's China, it is certain that the costs will be very low and the benefits will be high" (12: 21).

He saw the comparative advantage of China in terms of production cost, but he neglected China's comparative disadvantages in technology and the necessary conditions (such as military power and administrative supports) that European mercantilism was heavily relied upon.

The second argument is the exploitation by advanced countries: due to over population, low wage level and inefficiency in production and administration, the profit rate of Chinese firms and producers are low. On the other hand, the high price and wage rate level made Western countries "suffered from overly high wage and overly low profit rates."

The investments of Western countries in China "are not for the improvement of our wage rate, their real intention is to earn profits. Recently foreign investments increased significantly, very many laborers came to ask for employment, ... but what we gained is this small part of wage share, and a major part of profit was gained by foreigners. ...It makes me trembling when thinking of our future" (12: 33). This is

---

[3] Wang and Trescott 1989:75 mistranslated this note.

a commonly observed phenomenon even in today's developing countries. This is a common observation, not an insight.

Summaries

The lengthy Chap. 9 (12: 28–43) is to summarize Smith's ideas, excepted for one page on his life and work. The previous chapters were either on a school or on a long period of time, why this chapter devoted to a single person, one single book, with details and longest pages?

First, "This it the only book of this kind in Chinese language (the one or two already existed are not significant). But it is not accessible for general readers for its difficult style. My summaries may help readers to have a basic and essential ideas" (12: 1). Second, WN is more systematic than other books of this kind, he emphasized more on policy issues. Third, Yan Fu's difficult style did not trouble Liang; on the contrary, Yan's translation in classic style is convenient for Liang to rewrite for general readers. Fourth, it is a good opportunity for Liang to read this book carefully and "summarize its essential ideas for interested readers."

Liang's summaries contained 16 pages; they are only a very small part of Yan Fu's three volumes; it is very incomplete, and there is no systematic lines of thought that can be traced.

(1) Book I was summarized in pp. 30–5, in which only the division of labor, nature price, market price, rent, wage, profit were mentioned. Book I contains 11 chapters; it is sweepingly reviewed in six pages. Liang was conscious about this: "It is certainly difficult to summarize all these ideas in a bi-monthly popular magazine, a bit more detail summary may need 20 or 30 issues to cover" (12: 1).
(2) The same is true for Book II that Liang summarized in four pages (12: 35–9).
(3) Only three lines were devoted to Book III. Liang's statement in the final sentence reads: "On the one hand Smith emphasized on the study of history, but on the other hand he emphasized on the nature order of things. There is something in conflict between the two, as have been criticized by later scholars. We need not to quote them" (12: 39).
(4) What is arguable is his summary of Book IV. A key message in this Book is that Smith criticized mercantile system for their monopoly and interventionism, upon which Smith advocated the famous laissez-faire idea. Liang used a few lines on Smith's idea that free trade is beneficial for all trading countries (12: 41–2), but Liang's main target was to restate Smith's attack of bullionism: it is fallacious to consider bullion as the wealth of nation, money is simply a medium of exchange and should not be regarded as the wealth itself.

Having criticized mercantilism's idea of bullion, Liang began to write a long Appendix on "The principle of balance of payments and its relevance to Chinese economy" (pp. 43–61). For Liang, China's deficits in the balance of payments is a more urgent issue than economic liberalism.

(5) By that time the most urgent problem was (foreign) debts, and that is the main subject of Book V. Yan Fu offered many strong comments on this issue but Liang stopped at Book IV, which was appeared in an 1904 issue of the magazine, three years before its closed down.

In short, Liang summarized the first four Books of WN in a sweeping way, missed the central message of Smithian liberalism and omitted Book V which is mostly related to China's urgent situation.

Conclusion

Reading Liang's "Concise History" a century later, an overall impression is that the contents he translated/rendered are basically sound, a main difficulty of modern readers is the terminology that Yan Fu and Liang used. His comments are also reasonable excepted for his idea that China should adopt the European mercantile system: he over-simplified the necessary conditions to warrant a successful mercantilism in the world market. He also missed Smith's ideas about national debt.

Many intellectuals were influenced by Liang's popular magazine, which served as an important window to Western minds. Liang's style and insights were an attractive magnetic in that time. Many intellectuals learned the existence of history of economic thought through Liang's "Concise History," many began to read Yan Fu's WN after reading Liang's summary. In retrospect, Liang was a famous "guide to WN" as he claimed to be, although occasionally he missed some essential messages.[4]

---

[4] Wang and Trescott pp. 55–73 translated Liang's Chap. 9 "Adam Smith's Theory of Economics" into English, from which interested readers may also want to know how Liang's text is related to Luigi Cossa and John Kells Ingram's ideas.

References

Alexandrin, G. (1977). Reception of Adam Smith's *The Wealth of Nations* in early Russia. *Social Science Forum, 1*(1), 1–13.
Blaug, M. (1997). *Economic theory in retrospect* (5th ed.). Cambridge University Press.
Chen, J.-G. (2017). Yan Fu's Wealth of Nations: A Victorian Adam Smith in Late Qing China. *Adam Smith Review, 9*, 146–168.
Clough, S., & Rapp, R. (1975). *European economic history* (3rd ed.). McGraw-Hill.
Eichengreen, B. (1992). *Golden fetters: the gold standard and the great depression, 1919–1939*. Oxford University Press.
Ekelund, R., & Hébert, R. (1997). *A history of economic theory and method*. McGraw-Hill.
Hsu, I. (1983). *The rise of modern China* (3rd ed.). Oxford University Press.
Irwin, D. (2015). *Free trade under fire* (4th ed.). Princeton University Press.
Lai, C. (1989). Adam Smith and Yan Fu: Western economics in Chinese perspective. *Journal of European Economic History, 18*(2), 371–381.
Lai, C. (1996a). Translations of *The Wealth of Nations*. *Journal of European Economic History, 25*(2), 467–500.
Lai, C. (1996b). Receptions of *The Wealth of Nations*. *The European Legacy, 1*(7), 2069–2083.
Lai, C. (Ed.). (2000). *Adam Smith Across Nations: Translations and Receptions of* The Wealth of Nations. Oxford University Press, Oxford.
List, F. (1841). *The national system of political economy*, translated by Sampson Lloyd (1916), London: Longmans, Green & Co. Chapter 31: The system of values of exchange (falsely termed by the school, the 'industrial' system)—Adam Smith (pp. 277–281).
Luo, W. (2017). Adam Smith Scholarship in People's Republic of China, 1949–2013. *Adam Smith Review, 9*, 237–251.
Palyi, M. (1928). The introduction of Adam Smith on the continent. In J. M. Clark et al. (Eds.). *Adam Smith, 1776–1926* (pp. 190–233). University of Chicago Press. Augustus Kelley 1966 reprint, New York.
Ross, I. (2010). *The life of Adam Smith* (2nd ed.). Oxford University Press.
Schwartz, B. (1964). *In search of wealth and power: Yen Fu and the West*. Harvard University Press.
Smith, A. (1776). *An inquiry into the nature and causes of the wealth of nations*. Oxford University Press. The Glasgow editions of the Works and Correspondence of Adam Smith, edited by Campbell and Skinner, 1976.
Wang, Z., & P. Trescott (1988). *Liang Chi-chao and the introduction of Western economic ideas into China*. Southern Illinois University at Carbondale, Department of Economics discussion paper series 88–6.
Zhu, S. (1993). Adam Smith in China. In Mizuta & Sugiyama (Eds.), *Adam Smith: International perspectives* (pp. 279–291). Macmillan, London.

Chinese and Japanese References

艾约瑟(1892–6)(富国养民策),《万国公报》第43–88册。选录于李天纲(1998)编《万国公报文选》, 北京: 三联 (页535–46)。
曹旭华 (1986)(严复的富国论与亚当·斯密的《国富论》),《经济问题探索》, 第7期。
陈文亮 (1994)(严复经济思想探索),《理论学习月刊》, 第3–4期。
郭大力、王亚南(1931)译《国富论》, 中华书局(上下册)。1972–4年修订后改名《国民财富的性质和原因的研究》, 北京: 商务印书馆(上下册)。
郭湛波 (1973)(严复),《近代中国思想史》香港: 龙门书店, 页9–61。
郭正昭 (1978)《严复》, 台北: 商务印书馆。
侯厚吉、吴其敬(1983)(严复的经济思想),《中国近代经济思想史稿》第二册, 黑龙江: 人民出版社, 页506–69。
侯家驹 (1982)《中国经济思想史》, 台北: 中央文物供应社。
胡寄窗 (1962, 1963, 1981)《中国经济思想史》, 上海: 人民出版社(三册)。
胡寄窗 (1982)《中国近代经济思想史大纲》, 北京: 中国社会科学出版社, 第十章(严复的经济思想), 页212–35。
黄克武 (1998)《自由的所以然: 严复对约翰弥尔自由思想的认识与批判》, 台北: 允晨。
黄克武 (1998a)(严复研究的新趋向: 记近年来三次有关严复的研讨会),《近代中国史研究通讯》, 25:1–19。
赖建诚 (1989)(亚当史密斯与严复:《国富论》与中国),《汉学研究》, 7(2):303–40。
李泽厚 (1977)(论严复), 原载于《历史研究》1977年第2期, 辑入《中国近代思想史论》, 页290–333, 台北: 谷风出版社(1986)。
梁启超 (1902)(绍介新著: 原富),《新民丛报》1:113–5。
林保淳 (1988)《严复: 中国近代思想启蒙者》, 台北: 幼狮书局。
林其泉 (1993)(简议严复对《原富》的翻译),《中国社会经济史研究》, 4: 88–92。
林载爵 (1983)(严复对自由的理解),《历史学报》(台中: 东海大学) , 5:85–159。
刘富本 (1977) 编著《严复的富强思想》, 台北: 文景出版社。
刘瑾玉 (2021)(翻译、概念与经济: 严复译《国富论》研究》, 北京: 社会科学文献出版社。
刘重焘 (1985)(严复翻译《原富》之经过),《华东师范大学报》(社科版) , 60:94–6 (页97附严译英文底本书影与严注手迹)。
罗耀九 (1978)(严复的经济思想评述),《中国经济问题》, 第2期。
牛仰山、孙鸿霓 (1990) 编《严复研究资料》, 福州: 海峡文艺出版社。
欧阳哲生 (1994)《严复评传》, 南昌: 百花州文艺。
皮后锋 (2000)(《原富》的翻译与传播: 兼与赖建诚教授商榷),《汉学研究》, 18(1):309–30。
森时彦 (2001)(梁启超的经济思想),《梁启超·明治日本·西方》, 北京: 社会科学文献出版社, 页218–43。日文版: (梁啓超の經濟思想), 收錄於狹間直樹(1999)編《梁啓超: 西洋近代思想と明治日本》, 東京: みすず書房, 頁229–54。
史全生 (1978)(论严复的经济思想),《南京大学学报》(社科) , 3: 60–70。
手代木有儿 (1994)(严复の英国留学: その軌跡と西洋認識),《中国–社会と文化》, 9:170–86。
舒扬 (1982)(严复人口思想评述),《福建论坛》, 第6期。
汪荣祖 (1994)(严复的翻译),《中国文化》, 9:117–23。
王方中 (1982)《中国近代经济史稿: 1840–1927》, 北京出版社。
王栻 (1975)《严复传》, 上海: 人民出版社。
王栻 (1986) 编《严复集》, 北京: 中华书局 (五册)。
王栻、王佐良 (1982) 编《论严复与严译名著》, 北京: 商务印书馆。
王中江 (1997)《严复》, 台北: 东大图书公司。
严复 (1902) 译《原富》, 台北: 商务印书馆, 人人文库, 特506–8, 三册 (1977)。
严复专集: 严复著述及研究文献全文光盘(2000), 北京大学未名文化公司 (二十世纪中国文化史·著名学者光盘数据库系列)。
严扬 (1997)(新发现的严复增删《原富》未完稿),《中国文化》, 15–16合刊号, 页359–64。
叶世昌 (1980)(从《原富》按语看严复的经济思想),《经济研究》, 第7期。

References

俞政 (1994)(论严复的经济自由主义),《苏州大学学报》,第3期。另刊于《93年严复国际学术研讨会论文集》,福州: 海峡文艺出版社, 1995年页384–97。
俞政 (1995)(析严译《原富》按语中的国富策),《苏州大学学报》,第3期。
俞政 (1997)(严译《原富》的社会反应), 福州: 1997年严复与中国近代化研讨会论文。
张守军 (1999)(严复的经济思想),《财经问题研究》, 10:71–5。
张志建 (1989)《严复思想研究》,桂林: 广西师范大学。
张志建 (1995)《严复学术思想研究》,北京: 商务印书馆。
赵丰田 (1939)《晚清五十年经济思想史》, 台北: 华世出版社 (影印)。
赵靖、易梦虹 (1980) 编《中国近代经济思想史》, 下册, 页344–57 (严复)。
赵靖、易梦虹 (1982)《中国近代经济思想资料选辑》,北京: 中华书局(三册)。
周宪文、张汉裕 (1964) 译《国富论》上下册,台湾银行: 经济学名著翻译丛书第二种。
周振甫 (1936) 编《严复思想述评》,台北: 中华书局 (1987年重印)。

GPSR Compliance

The European Union's (EU) General Product Safety Regulation (GPSR) is a set of rules that requires consumer products to be safe and our obligations to ensure this.

If you have any concerns about our products, you can contact us on

ProductSafety@springernature.com

In case Publisher is established outside the EU, the EU authorized representative is:

Springer Nature Customer Service Center GmbH
Europaplatz 3
69115 Heidelberg, Germany